JOURNEY THROUGH

SCIENCE

JOURNEY THROUGH

SCIENCE

DOUGLAS McTAVISH

HAMLYN

Editors: Beryl Creek and Julie Good
Designer: Mark Summersby
Picture Researcher: Anna Smith
Production: Linda Spillane

Published in 1992 by
Hamlyn Children's Books,
part of Reed International Books,
Michelin House, 81 FulhamRoad,
London SW3 6RB

ISBN 0 600 57371 0

Printed in Italy

CONTENTS

THE NATURE OF MATTER

Everything on earth and in the universe around us consists of what we call matter. All matter is made up of tiny building blocks called atoms, which sometimes join together in groups called molecules. These atoms and molecules also join together to form elements and compounds. An element contains atoms of just one type - pure gold, for example, contains only gold atoms. Compounds are combinations of different elements, and so they are made from atoms of two or more types. Common salt is a compound made by mixing sodium and chlorine atoms.

In any substance, each atom or molecule is attracted to the other atoms and molecules around it by what are called electromagnetic forces. If you rest your elbow on something hard, such as a table, your arm does not sink in because these forces hold the atoms in the table close together.

However, atoms and molecules are moving all the time. They vibrate constantly, travelling a tiny distance in one direction, then in another, and so on. Sometimes they move faster and sometimes slower, and the forces between them can become weaker or stronger; when these factors change, the way in which matter behaves changes too.

Solids, Liquids and Gases

Matter takes many forms, but it comes in three basic states - solid, liquid and gas. In a solid, the atoms or molecules are vibrating relatively slowly. Also, they are very close together and the forces between them are strong. This is what gives many solids their strength and hardness. Solids in which the forces are weak are not as hard as those with strong forces. Examples of this are diamond and graphite (the "lead" in pencils), both of which are solids made up of carbon atoms. In diamond, an extremely hard material, the forces between the atoms are very strong. In graphite, however, the carbon atoms are in layers which lie one on top of another. The forces between layers are not very strong and the layers can slide over each other quite easily, which makes graphite weak.

Diamond, graphite and most other solids are made up of crystals - small pieces of material with straight edges and flat sides. Sugar and salt are well-known crystals. If you looked through a powerful microscope at steel you would see that it, too, consists of crystals.

The forces between atoms or molecules in a liquid are weaker than those in a solid. Because of this, liquids can flow from place to place. However, the forces are strong enough to resist flow, and this resistance is called viscosity. Liquids with high viscosity, such as treacle, flow slowly while those with low viscosity, such as water, flow more quickly.

Unlike solids, liquids do not have a definite shape - they take the shape of whatever container they are in. When a liquid is still, its surface is perfectly level. Another property of liquids is that some substances, including solids, gases and other liquids, will dissolve in them, forming what are called solutions.

Below: When steel is magnified hundreds of times, we can see that it is made up of crystals.

The atoms or molecules in a gas are vibrating extremely fast, so fast that the forces between them cannot hold them together. Many gases, including air, are impossible to see because their molecules are far apart. They are also very easy to compress, or squeeze. Like liquids, gases can flow, but other substances will not dissolve in them. One gas will mix with another in a process called diffusion.

Changing State

Some substances are familiar to us in all three states. Water is a good example; normally it is a liquid, but we also know it as a solid, ice, and as a gas, steam. The state it is in depends upon the temperature. It becomes solid when we cool it down to 0°C and turns into a gas when heated to 100°C. When water is heated, the molecules move faster and faster until, at 100°C (boiling point), they break the forces between them and the water becomes a gas. When cooled, the molecules vibrate slower and slower until, at 0°C (freezing point), the forces between them are strong enough to hold the water together as a solid. Many other substances can be made to change state by heating or cooling them.

Below: Whether a substance is solid, liquid or gaseous depends on the amount of energy its atoms or molecules contain.

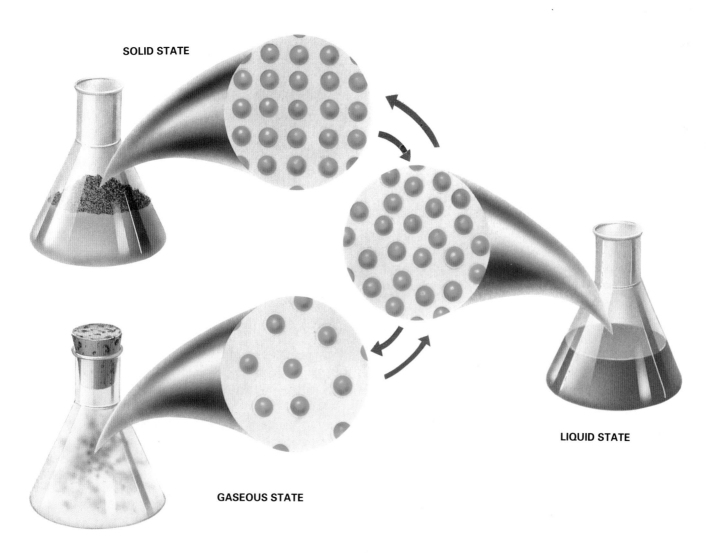

SOLID STATE

GASEOUS STATE

LIQUID STATE

INSIDE THE ATOM

Left: Ernest Rutherford (right) showed that all atoms contain electrons in orbit around a central nucleus.

Since the time of the ancient Greeks, many scientists have believed that all matter is made up of atoms. However, the first real evidence that atoms actually exist did not come until 1802. In that year, the Englishman John Dalton was able to measure the mass of certain atoms and to explain how they joined together to form molecules. Like the Greeks, Dalton thought atoms were the smallest particles that could exist, and he pictured them as being like very small billiard balls.

Christmas Puddings, Clouds and Shells

In 1875 another English scientist, J. J. Thomson, suggested that atoms contained even smaller particles, called electrons, dotted about like currants in a Christmas pudding. Some years later Ernest Rutherford showed that all atoms contained electrons, which he thought circled in a cloud around a dense region at the centre, called the nucleus. In 1913 Neils Bohr said that the electrons orbited around the nucleus in a series of layers, or shells, rather like planets circling the Sun.

In fact, the paths followed by electrons as they fly around the nucleus of an atom are much more complicated than Bohr imagined. When electrons are passed through a narrow slit they appear to spread out in a wave. This means that, inside an atom, it is impossible to predict exactly where an electron might be at any moment. So, instead of placing them in precise orbits, scientists now draw three-dimensional maps of electron "orbitals" showing where they are likely to be. The four simplest orbital shapes are a sphere, a dumb-bell, a four-leaf clover, and an hourglass and ring. Others are too complicated to draw.

Inside the Nucleus

The proton, one of the building blocks which make up the nucleus, was first discovered in 1886. Each proton carries a positive electric charge, and the number of protons in an atom is balanced by an equal number of negatively charged electrons. The next particle to be discovered inside the nucleus was the neutron, which was identified by James Chadwick in 1932. Neutrons have no electric charge. Other particles have since been discovered using what are called particle accelerators. Inside these machines, particles such as electrons and neutrons are accelerated to very high speeds and fired at atomic nuclei. If an accelerated particle scores a direct hit on a nucleus, other particles are produced. These new particles can survive for only a very short time, and so the tracks they make must be recorded very

DALTON'S THEORY 1802 • ELECTRON 1875 • PROTON 1886 • EINSTEIN'S PHOTON 1905

ELECTRON ORBITALS

When electrons were first discovered, scientists thought that these tiny particles moved around the nuclei of atoms in a sort of cloud, or that they orbited in layers. In fact, the exact path of an electron is far too complex to work out. Modern scientists use three-dimensional maps to show electron orbitals - regions in which electrons are likely to be found. These are the four simplest orbital shapes: there are others that are so complicated they are almost impossible to draw.

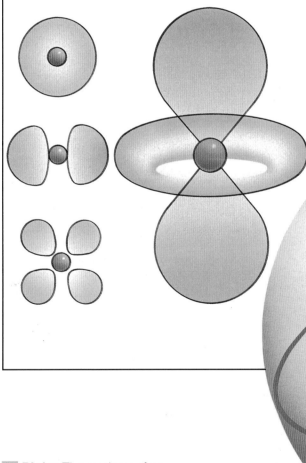

quickly using special detectors.

New particles found in this way include muons, taus, and neutrinos (known collectively as leptons), pions and kaons (so-called composite particles) and quarks. It seems that protons, neutrons and some other composite particles are made up of a number of quarks. There are now thought to be six different types of quark, which have been christened Up, Down, Strange, Charm, Bottom and Top.

As well as these leptons, quarks and composite particles, there is another group called bosons. One of them, the photon, is a particle of light which was first suggested by Albert Einstein in 1905. Another boson is called the gluon; experiments carried out in 1982 seem to prove their existence but they have never been seen. Even more mysterious are gravitons, which are thought to be gravity particles although there is, as yet, no evidence that they exist.

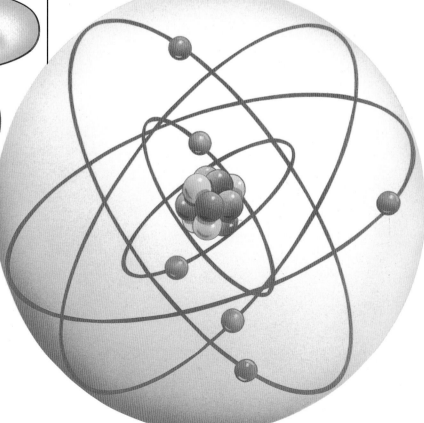

Right: The nucleus of an atom consists of protons and neutrons. Electrons orbit around the nucleus. This is a carbon atom, with 6 electrons and 6 protons.

FORCES AND MOTION

A force is something that affects the shape and motion of an object. There are four main types of force: electric, magnetic, nuclear and gravitational. Electric force acts between two electrically charged particles (pp. 8-9). A force between two moving electric charges is called a magnetic force (pp. 44-5). (The electromagnetic forces which hold atoms and molecules together are a combination of these two forces.) Nuclear forces exist between the tiny particles inside the nucleus of an atom (pp. 8-9). Gravitational force is the attraction between any two objects which have mass (pp. 12-13). When you push or pull an object you are applying a force; this type of force is related to gravitational force.

The study of the relationship between the motion of an object and the forces acting upon it is called dynamics. Among the first people to think about the way in which things move, and why, were the ancient Greeks, whose civilization was at its height between the sixth and third centuries BC. They believed that every object in the universe had its own special place, and that things moved to get back to where they belonged. The natural place for rocks to be was on the earth, so if one was lifted up and dropped it would fall downwards.

Galileo and Newton

The teachings of the Greeks, especially those of a man called Aristotle, went unchallenged for almost 2,000 years. In 1591, a scientist called Galileo Galilei discovered that objects move simply because they are pushed or pulled by forces.

Galileo did not know what the forces are. The problem was solved in 1687 by Isaac Newton. In his book, *Principia*, he set out his three laws of motion which explained how forces act to make things move. He also showed that one special force, gravitation, acted throughout the whole Universe (see the chapter on Gravity). In honour of this great scientist's work, all forces are now measured in units called newtons.

Friction and Centripetal Force

When you kick a ball across the ground, it doesn't carry on moving for ever. It slows down gradually and eventually stops. From Newton's laws of motion we know that this is because there is a force acting on the ball causing it to slow down. This force is called friction and it acts when two surfaces rub together. Without the friction between our feet and the ground we would not be able to walk along.

If you tie a conker at one end of a length of string and whirl it around your head, it follows a circular path. The direction in which it moves changes all the time which, according to Newton, means that a force must be acting upon it. This force acts through the string. If the string broke, the force would stop acting and the conker would fly off through the air in a straight line. The force that causes the circular motion of the conker is called centripetal force, and it acts towards the centre of the circle. It is sometimes, though mistakenly, called centrifugal force.

Below: Centripetal force keeps this athlete's hammer moving in a circle.

NEWTON'S LAWS OF MOTION

The First Law of Motion states that an object will stay still or continue moving at the same speed in a straight line unless a force acts upon it. This idea, first suggested by Galileo, is called inertia. A large ship such as an oil tanker, moving at a steady speed, has so much inertia that it must begin slowing down a long way before it needs to stop.

Newton's Second Law says that a moving object moves faster, or accelerates, when acted on by a force. It accelerates in the direction of the force, and the amount of acceleration depends on the size of the force and the mass of the object - how much matter it contains. That is why a heavy stone is more difficult to throw than a lighter one.

The Third Law of Motion says that forces act in pairs. When you push or pull an object, it pushes or pulls back with an equal force. Athletes take advantage of this when they use starting blocks for races; when they push against the blocks, the blocks push back with an equal force, and propel the runners forward.

Right: This magnified view shows why there is friction between surfaces when we try to move one over another. Where they touch, forces between their molecules hold them together

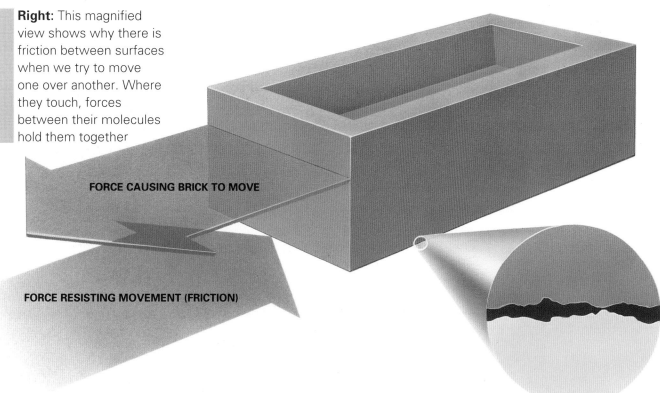

FORCE CAUSING BRICK TO MOVE

FORCE RESISTING MOVEMENT (FRICTION)

GRAVITY

Why is it that we are able to walk around the Earth without flying off into space? Why doesn't the Moon crash into our planet or veer off into the universe? To the ancient Greeks, the answer was clear: humans, the Moon and the Earth are all in their natural places.

Newton and Universal Gravitation

Galileo's experiments of the 1590s told him that objects moved when forces acted upon them, but he didn't know what the forces were. As we have seen, the problem was solved by Isaac Newton. It is said that he was sitting in an orchard one day when an apple fell to the ground. He realized that the Earth must be pulling the apple towards it. This started him thinking about other objects in the universe, and he calculated that they were all attracted to each other by a single force, gravity. It is gravity that holds the Moon in its orbit and keeps us on the surface of the Earth. Gravity is what gives us weight. We all have mass - the more matter we contain,

the greater is our mass. Weight is the downward force which is exerted on us by gravity, and so the more mass we have, the more we weigh.

Newton's studies showed that if you travel away from the Earth, the force of gravity gradually becomes weaker. This is because the gravitational pull between two objects depends upon how far apart they are. In fact, gravity decreases as the square of the distance between the objects increases, so if you double the distance, the pull between them is one quarter of what

Below: Isaac Newton may have first thought about gravity when he watched an apple fall from a tree.

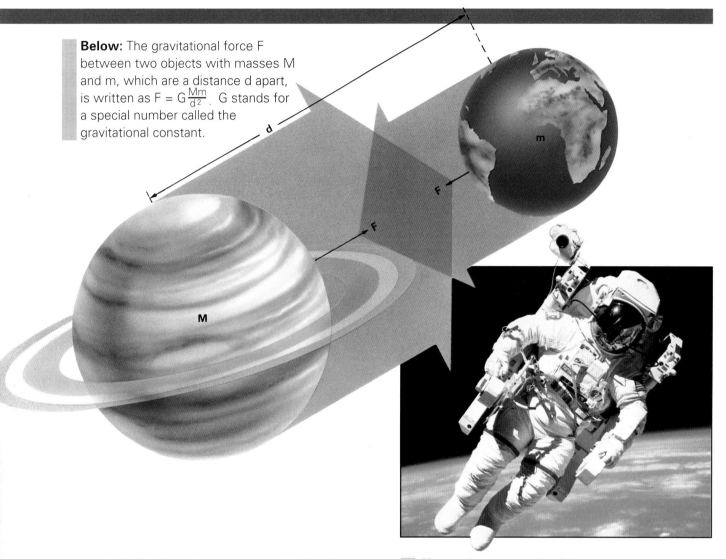

Below: The gravitational force F between two objects with masses M and m, which are a distance d apart, is written as $F = G\frac{Mm}{d^2}$. G stands for a special number called the gravitational constant.

Above: A person on the Moon experiences less gravitational force than on the Earth.

it was originally. As we have seen, gravitational attraction is also affected by the mass of the objects. Because the Moon's mass is only one sixth as much as the Earth's, its gravitational pull is one-sixth of that on Earth. If you can jump 1 m into the air on Earth, you would be able to jump 6 m on the Moon.

Einstein and Gravitational Waves

In 1915 a German-born scientist, Albert Einstein, published his General Theory of Relativity. According to this theory, the force of gravity is different from the other types of force we experience on Earth. Einstein said that the vast area of space, in which the stars and planets exist, is not the same everywhere. In some places around stars with a very high mass space is actually curved, and this is what causes gravity. For example, the Sun curves the space around it and forces the Earth to travel along a curved path.

In Einstein's theory the attraction between two bodies, such as the Earth and the Sun, moves in waves. These gravitational waves are very weak and no one has yet been able to prove they exist on Earth. However, when astronomers looked closely at a large star far out in space, called PSR 1913+ 16, they were able to show that it was giving off gravitational waves. Thanks to these observations and other experiments, the General Theory of Relativity is now accepted by most scientists.

FLUIDS

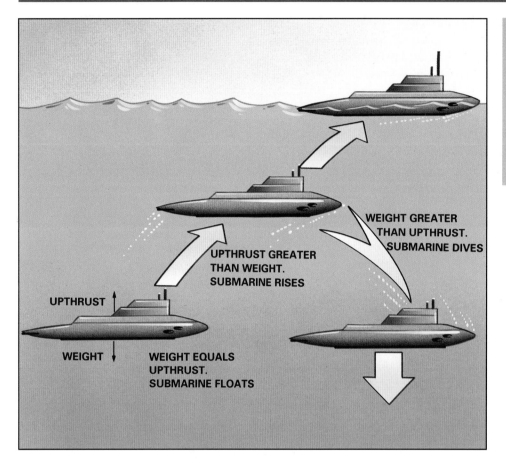

UPTHRUST

WEIGHT

WEIGHT EQUALS UPTHRUST. SUBMARINE FLOATS

UPTHRUST GREATER THAN WEIGHT. SUBMARINE RISES

WEIGHT GREATER THAN UPTHRUST. SUBMARINE DIVES

Left: When the weight of a submarine is equal to the upthrust on it, the submarine floats under-water. When it is heavier it sinks, and when it is lighter, it rises. The weight is adjusted by changing the amounts of air and water in its ballast tanks.

Have you ever noticed that you feel lighter when you are in the bath? This is because you actually weigh less when you are immersed in water, even though your mass remains exactly the same as it was before you got into the bath.

Archimedes' Principle

The first person to think about this was a Greek scientist called Archimedes, who lived more than 2,000 years ago. He discovered that when an object is placed in a fluid (a liquid or a gas) it displaces or moves aside some of the fluid, and the object's weight is reduced. The apparent loss in weight is equal to the weight of the displaced fluid.

A person in a bath or any other solid object immersed in a fluid weighs less than in the air because the water pushes up on them with what is called an upthrust. To put Archimedes' Principle another way, the upthrust on an object is equal to the weight of fluid it displaces.

Pressure, Density and Surface Tension

The upthrust on an immersed object is caused by pressure within the fluid. Pressure is the force acting upon the object divided by the area of the object. The deeper you go in a fluid, the greater the pressure, so the pressure at the bottom of an immersed object is higher than at the top. The difference in pressure produces an upthrust on the object.

The pressure in a fluid also depends upon the density of the fluid: its weight divided by its volume (the amount of space it takes up). A litre of air weighs much less than a litre of water, so we say that air is less dense than water. If an object is placed in a fluid that is more dense, it will float. For example, ice is only about nine-tenths as dense as water, so an ice cube floats with about 90 per cent of it underwater.

The air around us is a fluid and so it exerts a pressure, which we call atmospheric pressure. One of the first people to prove this was Evangelista Torricelli who, in

1643, invented a device called a barometer in which atmospheric pressure forced mercury to rise inside a glass tube. The height to which it rose depended upon the pressure of the atmosphere. As we know, pressure varies with depth, and so the atmospheric pressure at the earth's surface - at the bottom of the atmosphere - is greater than at the top of a mountain.

There are many animals that can float in water, and some that can even walk on it. Small insects, such as pond skaters, are able to walk across the surface of a pond without getting their feet wet. They can do this because of something called surface tension.

Water is made up of molecules, held together by forces between them. At the surface, this causes water to act almost as though it is covered with a thin rubber skin. The surface tension is strong enough to support the weight of pond skaters. It also explains why rain falls in rounded drops; the molecules nearest the outside of the drops are pulled inwards towards the centre of the liquid.

Right: We feel lighter in a fluid because of the upward force, or upthrust, exerted by the fluid.

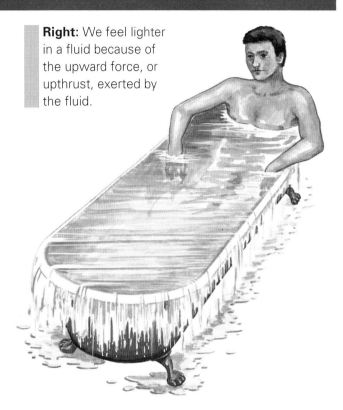

Below: Water flowing from holes in a cylinder shows how pressure in a fluid increases with depth.

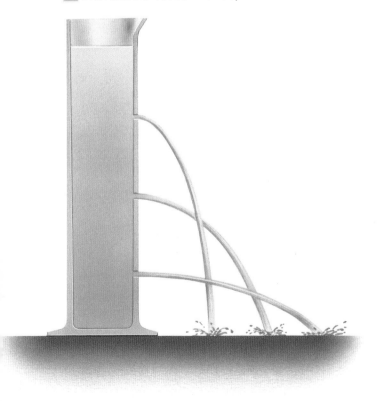

Below: Although it is more dense than water, this razor blade "floats" because of surface tension.

ELASTICITY

If you hold a rubber band with both hands and pull it, the band stretches and then returns to its normal length when you stop pulling it. However, if you pull hard enough the band will eventually break.

The same thing happens when a weight is hung from the end of a length of wire. At first, the wire stretches slightly, but it returns to normal when the weight is removed. This is called elastic stretching. If a heavier weight is used, the wire will stretch but will not return to normal. If the weight is increased even more, the wire will become what is called "plastic", and will stretch very rapidly and then break.

Hooke's Law

In 1676 an English scientist, Robert Hooke, discovered the law that governs the way in which solid materials stretch. He found that the amount of stretching, or extension, of a wire is directly linked to the weight attached to it, but only up to a certain point. If the weight is increased beyond that point, called the elastic limit, the wire will not return to its normal length but will stay stretched.

It is sometimes very important to know what the elastic limit of a material is. Suspension bridges are often held up by thick wires hung from curved metal

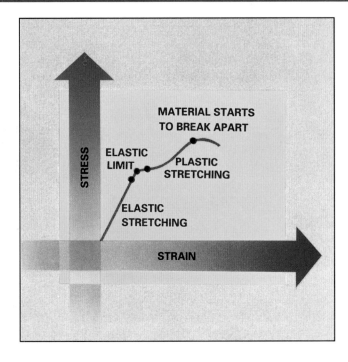

Above: A graph of the stress (force) on a material against strain (how much it stretches). **Below:** The wires of a suspension bridge must be able to carry a heavy load.

HOOKE'S LAW 1676 • STRETCHING INVOLVES PULLING ATOMS AWAY FROM EACH OTHER

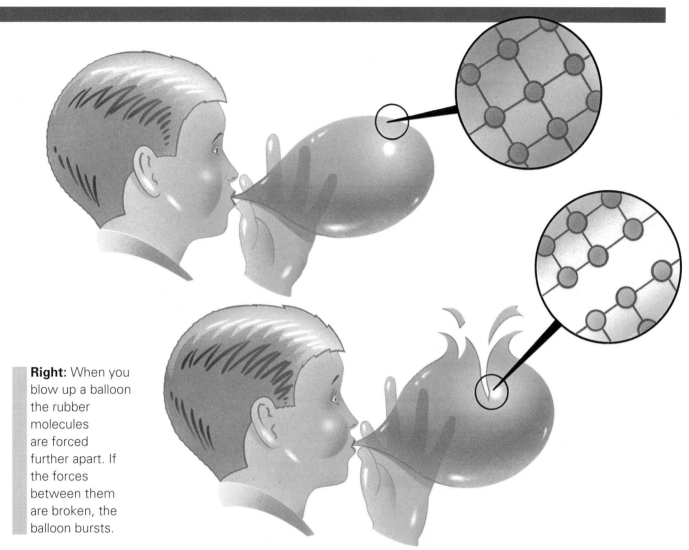

Right: When you blow up a balloon the rubber molecules are forced further apart. If the forces between them are broken, the balloon bursts.

rods that are attached to the tall towers at each end. The engineers who design these bridges have to know that the wires will be strong enough to bear the weight of the bridge and all the traffic it will carry.

Elasticity and Atoms

As we know, all materials are made up of atoms and molecules which are held together by electromagnetic forces. These forces are stronger in solids than in liquids or gases, but it is still possible to weaken them and pull the atoms apart. If you press too hard when you are writing with a pencil, you will break the point. The force you apply on the point is greater than the force holding the atoms together, and so the atoms separate and the "lead" breaks.

When a wire is stretched by a weight, what is really happening is the atoms in the wire are being pulled apart. If the wire isn't stretched too far, the forces between the atoms will pull them back together when the weight is removed. But if it is stretched beyond its elastic limit, the forces are made permanently weaker, and the atoms stay further apart. As a result, the wire remains longer than it was before being stretched. When the wire undergoes elastic stretching, the atoms are actually sliding over one another quite quickly.

All solids can be stretched but some won't stretch very far and they break shortly after their elastic limit is reached. Substances like this, such as glass, are called brittle. In contrast, some substances, such as copper, will stretch a long way beyond their elastic limit before breaking; they are called ductile substances.

ELASTICITY OF A MATERIAL DEPENDS UPON STRENGTH OF FORCES BETWEEN ATOMS

MACHINES

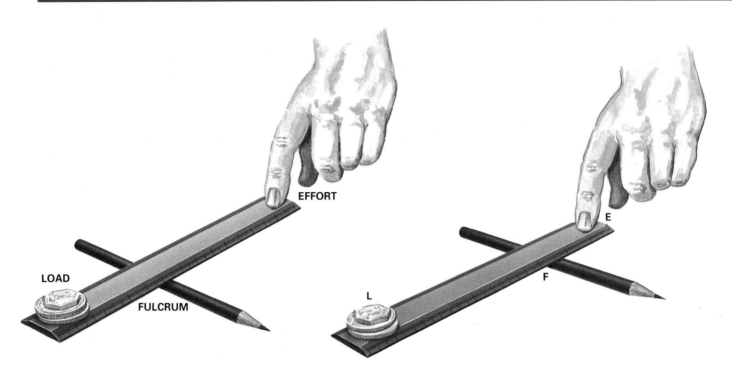

A machine is any device which is used to overcome a force. The force to be overcome is called the load, and when it is applied at one point the machine works by the application of another force, which is called the effort, applied at a different point. There are several different types of machines, including levers, pulleys, wheels and axles, wedges, inclined planes and screws.

Levers and Pulleys

A lever is a rigid object which pivots about a turning point, called the fulcrum, which does not move. If you lay a pencil on a table and rest a ruler across it, you have made a simple lever. The point where the ruler touches the pencil is the fulcrum. You can lift a weight (the load) placed on one end of the ruler by pushing down (applying an effort) on the other end.

Try moving the fulcrum closer to the load; you will find that less effort is needed to lift the load. If the fulcrum is close to the point where you apply the effort, the load is harder to lift. This is because the forces increase with their distance from the fulcrum. So, the longer the distance between the effort and the fulcrum, the greater the load that can be lifted. The Greek scientist Aristotle once said that if he had a long enough lever he could move the earth!

Above: A simple lever. An effort applied at one end can be used to lift a load at the other. Move the fulcrum to see what effect it has on the effort needed to lift the load.

When our ancient ancestors built monuments such as Stonehenge, they probably moved the enormous stones into position using strong logs as levers. Levers that are used every day include scissors, bottle openers and wheelbarrows.

We give levers different names depending upon where the fulcrum is and where the load and effort are applied. In a first-class lever, such as a crowbar, a pair of scissors or a seesaw, the effort and load are on opposite sides of the fulcrum. In a second-class lever, like a wheelbarrow or a bottle opener, the fulcrum is at one end and the load is closer to it than the effort. The fulcrum of a third-class lever, such as a pair of sugar tongs, is also at one end, but the effort is closer to the fulcrum than the load.

A pulley is another type of machine that can be used to lift loads. A string is wound over one or more pulley wheels, and when it is pulled a load is lifted. In most

ALL TYPES OF SIMPLE MACHINE OVERCOME LOAD BY APPLICATION OF EFFORT

cases, the more pulley wheels there are, the greater the load that can be lifted with the same effort.

Other Simple Machines

A wheel and axle is a machine used for supplying a turning force. A doorknob is one example. When a small force is applied to the knob, which moves around the axle in a circle, a much larger force is produced on the shaft which turns in a small circle.

An inclined plane is another type of machine. It is much easier to push a heavy object up a sloping plank than to lift it vertically. Logs can be split in half by hammering in a wedge - a machine which applies forces that push sideways.

Some major lifting tasks, such as raising a car to fit a new wheel, can be done using a screw jack. Turning the handle on the jack turns a screw to raise a load. Each complete turn of the handle lifts the load a distance known as the pitch, which is the distance between each thread on the screw.

Below: This type of pulley system, known as a block and tackle, is often used to lift heavy objects. It has several pulley wheels.

LEVERS

Levers are known as first-, second- or third-class depending upon the position of the fulcrum (the point about which the lever pivots) and the points at which the load (L) and effort (E) are applied. These illustrations show examples of the three classes of levers and how they work.

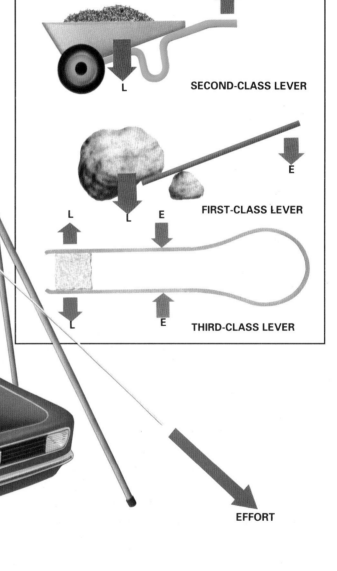

SECOND-CLASS LEVER

FIRST-CLASS LEVER

THIRD-CLASS LEVER

LOAD

EFFORT

ENERGY

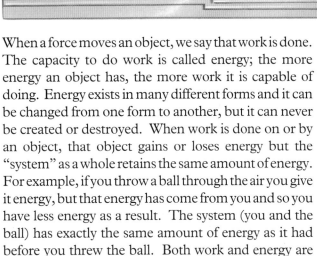

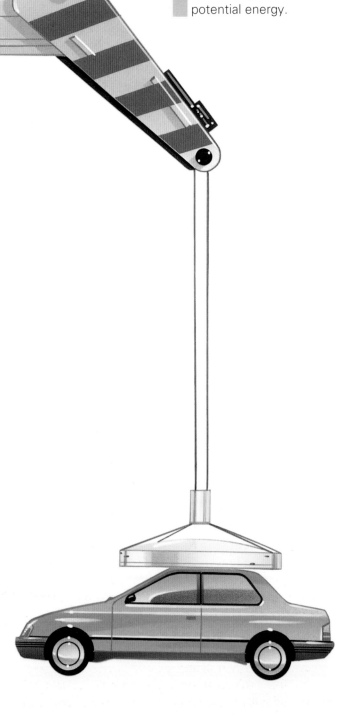

When a force moves an object, we say that work is done. The capacity to do work is called energy; the more energy an object has, the more work it is capable of doing. Energy exists in many different forms and it can be changed from one form to another, but it can never be created or destroyed. When work is done on or by an object, that object gains or loses energy but the "system" as a whole retains the same amount of energy. For example, if you throw a ball through the air you give it energy, but that energy has come from you and so you have less energy as a result. The system (you and the ball) has exactly the same amount of energy as it had before you threw the ball. Both work and energy are measured in units called joules.

Types of Energy

Scientists group all the different forms of energy into two types: potential energy and kinetic energy. Potential energy is the energy stored in an object or system because of its position, shape or state. The object or system possesses energy because work has been done on it to get it into that position, shape or state.

There are three forms of potential energy. The first of these, gravitational potential energy, is the energy an object has because of its position relative to another object which exerts a gravitational force upon it. If you pick up a stone from the ground, you are giving it gravitational potential energy because the stone is attracted by the earth's gravity. The higher you lift it, the more energy it has.

The second form, electromagnetic potential energy, is the energy of a body associated with its position relative to an electromagnetic force. An example of this is molecular potential energy, which is due to the positions of molecules relative to one another. If two molecules are moved further apart, work is done against the electromagnetic force holding them together, and so their molecular potential energy increases. Elastic potential energy, which is increased when you stretch something such as a rubber band, is a type of molecular

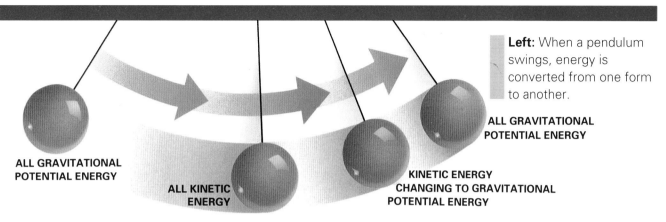

ALL GRAVITATIONAL
POTENTIAL ENERGY

ALL KINETIC
ENERGY

KINETIC ENERGY
CHANGING TO GRAVITATIONAL
POTENTIAL ENERGY

ALL GRAVITATIONAL
POTENTIAL ENERGY

Left: When a pendulum swings, energy is converted from one form to another.

potential energy. Another example of electromagnetic potential energy is chemical energy - the energy stored in fuels and food which is released during chemical reactions, such as when fuel burns or food is digested (see the chapters on Elements and Compounds).

The third form of potential energy is called nuclear potential energy. It is the energy stored inside the nucleus of an atom, and is released during radioactive decay (pp.48-9) and in nuclear fission and fusion (pp. 50-1).

The other main type of energy kinetic energy is associated with the movement of objects. Kinetic energy can be translational (moving from one place to another), rotational (spinning round), or vibrational (vibrating to and fro).

Energy Conversion

In many cases, objects have more than one type of energy at any one time. Imagine a swinging pendulum, for example. At the top of its swing, when it stops moving, it has gravitational potential energy and no kinetic energy; but when it starts to move downwards more and more of its energy is converted into kinetic energy, which reaches a maximum at the bottom of the swing. As it moves upwards again it slows down as kinetic energy is converted back into gravitational potential energy. The sum of an object's gravitational potential energy and its kinetic energy is called mechanical energy.

As we know, the atoms and molecules inside an object are always moving. They have both kinetic energy and molecular potential energy. The total energy (of both these types) of all of the atoms and molecules in an object is called the internal energy, or thermal energy.

Below: Rocket engines change chemical energy in fuel to kinetic and gravitational potential energy.

HEAT

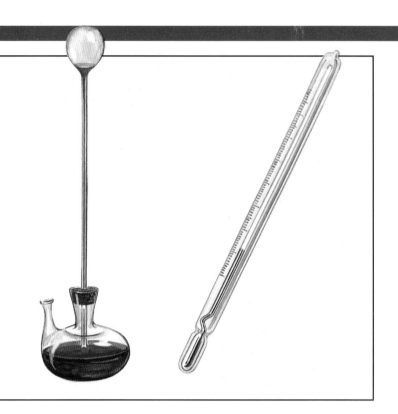

In the previous chapter we looked at energy and some of the forms in which it exists. One of the commonest forms of energy is heat.

Heat and Temperature

There is an important difference between heat and temperature. Temperature is a measure of the hotness or coldness of an object. Heat is the form of energy that flows from one place to another when there is a difference in temperature. When an object is heated its molecules are made to vibrate more rapidly; the heat energy is absorbed by the object and converted into kinetic energy. In this way the object's internal energy - the total energy of all its molecules - is increased. The amount of heat energy a body has depends upon the amount of matter it contains and on its temperature. Therefore, a large, cold object may contain more heat than a small, hot one.

We use thermometers to measure the temperature of things. The thermometer was invented around 1600. We do not know who made the first one, but Galileo certainly produced an air thermometer which he called a thermoscope. It worked on the principle that air (like most other things) expands and takes up more space as it becomes hotter. The first medical thermometer was made in 1626 by an Italian doctor, Santorio. The design was improved in 1867 by Thomas Allbutt. He used mercury as the liquid inside his thermometer, because it expands more than the water Santorio had used, making it easier to read accurately.

Temperature is measured in three scales. On the centigrade, or Celsius, scale, the temperature at which water freezes is 0°C, and that at which it boils is 100°C. On the Fahrenheit scale the freezing and boiling points of water are 32°F and 212°F. The lowest possible temperature on the Kelvin scale is zero Kelvin (0 K), or absolute zero. Scientists think that at this temperature all the molecules in an object stop moving, although no one has ever been able to cool anything down this far. One Kelvin is the same as 1°C; 0°C is 273 K on the Kelvin scale and 100°C is 373 K.

Heat is measured in units called calories. One calorie is the amount of heat needed to warm 1g of water through 1°C.

Latent Heat and Specific Heat Capacity

When an object melts or boils, it takes in heat but its temperature does not rise. Likewise, when it condenses or freezes it gives out heat without its temperature falling. This happens because when an object changes

state the energy it takes in or gives out is used to make or break the electromagnetic forces between the molecules. The heat energy taken in or given out when objects change state without changing their temperature is called latent heat. It was discovered in about 1763 by two scientists, Joseph Black and Johan Wilcke, working independently of each other.

The same two also studied what we call specific heat capacity. When hot objects made of different materials are dropped into cold water, they do not cause the temperature of the water to rise by the same amount even if they have the same mass and are at the same temperature to start with. For example, 100g of glass at 100°C gives out only one-fifth as much heat energy as 100g of water at the same temperature. The specific heat of water was set at 1 to give a standard by which other materials could be measured. So the specific heat of glass is one-fifth of that, or 0.2. This is caused by differing amounts of kinetic and molecular potential energy possessed by molecules in different substances.

Above: Joseph Black (1728-99), the Scottish chemist who discovered the principle of latent heat. Latent means "hidden".

Below: When a substance changes state from solid to liquid or liquid to gas, it takes in heat, but its temperature does not change.

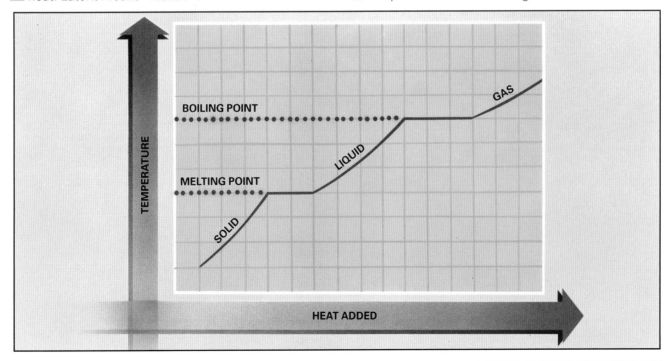

GASES

In a gas, the molecules are travelling extremely fast at about 1,600 km/h. They do not move very far because they are constantly bumping into one another.

The molecules are far too small for us to see, but we can sometimes see the effects of the collisions between them. If smoke particles in the air are studied under a microscope, they can be seen to make small, jerky movements. This motion, called Brownian motion after Robert Brown who first saw it in 1827, is caused by air molecules bumping into the smoke particles and pushing them in all directions.

Boyle's Law and Charles's Law

Gases are easy to squeeze together, or compress, because there is quite a lot of space between their molecules. In 1660 an Irish scientist, Robert Boyle, discovered that if a gas is squeezed so that the pressure on it is doubled, the space it occupies, its volume, is halved. If the volume of a set mass of gas is multiplied by its pressure, the result will always be the same.

Boyle's Law, as this discovery is called, is true only when the gas is kept at a steady temperature. As we saw in the previous chapter, most things expand when they are heated and contract when they are cooled. The link between the volume of a gas and its temperature was investigated by a French scientist, Jacques Charles, in 1798. He found that if a gas occupies a certain volume at 0°C, its volume will increase or decrease by 1/273 of that figure for each degree by which the temperature rises or falls. In the same way that Boyle's Law only applies when the temperature is constant, Charles's Law is only true if the pressure is kept constant. According to Charles's Law, if we could cool a gas down to absolute zero, -273.15°C, it would have no volume at all. Therefore, absolute zero must be the lowest possible temperature.

If all of the gas inside a hollow container could be removed, the empty space left would be called a total vacuum. The pressure inside the container would be zero and, unless the container was very strong, the pressure of the air outside would force it to collapse inwards. The first person to attempt to create a vacuum was a German engineer, Otto von Guericke. In 1654 he joined together two large metal hemispheres and pumped as much air as possible from the hollow space between them. He then harnessed horses to each

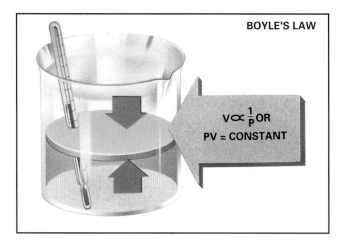

BOYLE'S LAW

$$V \propto \frac{1}{P} \text{ OR}$$
$$PV = \text{CONSTANT}$$

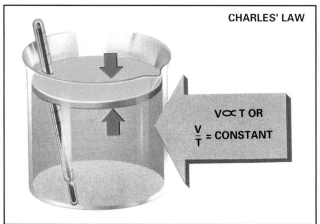

CHARLES' LAW

$$V \propto T \text{ OR}$$
$$\frac{V}{T} = \text{CONSTANT}$$

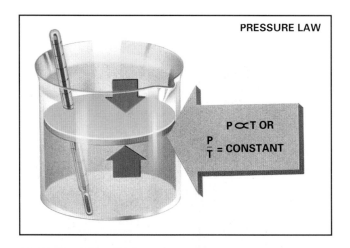

PRESSURE LAW

$$P \propto T \text{ OR}$$
$$\frac{P}{T} = \text{CONSTANT}$$

Above: The gas laws describe how gases behave in terms of pressure (P), volume (V) and temperature (T). $\propto$ means "is proportional to".

hemisphere and made them pull in opposite directions. The two hemispheres only came apart when eight horses were pulling on each.

Liquid Gases

If a gas is cooled down enough, it will eventually turn to liquid. The temperature at which a gas does this is called its critical temperature. Most of the elements that exist naturally as gases, so-called permanent gases including oxygen, nitrogen and hydrogen, have very low critical temperatures and so they are very difficult to liquify. Before the invention of modern deep-freezing techniques, scientists were unable to cool gases to these low temperatures.

However, in 1818 the English scientist Michael Faraday discovered a way of liquefying gases by increasing the pressure as he cooled them. He successfully made liquefied hydrogen sulphide and sulphuric anhydride, but he could not produce enough pressure to liquefy other so-called permanent gases. Louis-Paul Cailletet finally succeeded with oxygen in 1877, Karl von Linde liquefied air in 1899 and James Dewar produced liquid hydrogen in the same year.

Below: The experiment carried out by Otto von Guericke in 1654 to demonstrate a vacuum.

FARADAY LIQUEFIES GASES 1818 • BROWNIAN MOTION 1827 • LIQUID OXYGEN 1877

HEAT TRANSFER

Heat can move from one place to another. There are three ways in which it does this: by conduction, convection and radiation. Both conduction and convection can only occur if there is matter present, because they involve moving molecules. Radiation, however, can travel through empty space.

Conduction and Convection

When a solid object is heated, the molecules close to the source of the heat start to vibrate more rapidly than when the object is cool. They collide with molecules near them and pass on some of their energy. These collisions continue and eventually the whole object becomes heated. The process by which heat spreads through solid objects is called conduction. Some materials, especially metals, are good conductors of heat. Materials that do not conduct heat well, such as rubber, wood and glass, are called insulators.

Gases and liquids (except mercury, which is a molten metal) are bad conductors of heat. Heat travels through them in a different way to convection. When a saucepan of cold water is heated, the water near the heat source expands and becomes less dense, which causes it to rise. Cold water sinks to the bottom to take its place and in turn is heated, expands and rises. Warm water at or near the surface cools down, becomes more dense, and sinks. The movement of the heated water sets up currents, called convection currents.

In the earth's atmosphere, huge convection currents cause winds to blow. When the sun warms the earth, the air above the land is heated. As the warm air rises, cooler air rushes in to take its place. Convection currents in the oceans transfer heat from the hot regions around the equator to cooler parts of the world. On a smaller scale, many people use convection to heat their homes. For example, in a central heating system the so-called radiators are actually convectors, which set up convection currents in the air to carry heat around the rooms of a house.

Radiation

A great deal of heat comes to us directly from the sun in the form of radiation. It reaches us after travelling 150 million km through empty space. Heat radiation was discovered in 1800 by an English astronomer, William Herschel. He noticed that when sunlight is passed

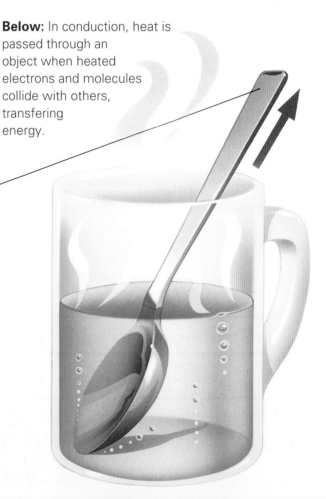

Below: In conduction, heat is passed through an object when heated electrons and molecules collide with others, transfering energy.

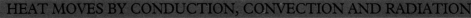

HEAT MOVES BY CONDUCTION, CONVECTION AND RADIATION

through a prism and split into its component colours, the red light gives off heat, which he detected with a thermometer. This happened because the light energy absorbed by the thermometer was converted into heat. Herschel also saw that the area just to one side of the beam of red light gave off heat. He concluded that the sun's rays carry energy other than light, and he named the rays of heat energy "infrared".

Infrared rays are similar to light rays, and they both travel at the same speed. They can be reflected, refracted (pp. 28-9) and absorbed. Shiny or light-coloured surfaces reflect heat better than dull or dark ones, and black objects absorb and radiate heat better than light-coloured ones.

Below: Convection currents in a heated saucepan of water. Hot water at the bottom rises, cools, sinks and is heated again.

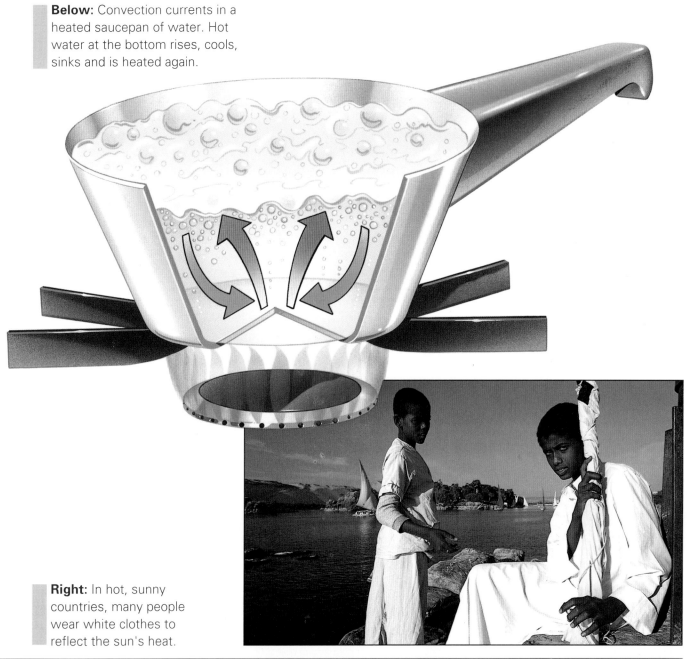

Right: In hot, sunny countries, many people wear white clothes to reflect the sun's heat.

LIGHT

The ancient Greeks thought that humans were able to see because their eyes gave out light that lit up objects in front of them, rather like the headlamps on a car. Like many of the Greeks' other scientific theories, this seemed to make common sense. However, it could not explain why things appear larger or smaller when they are moved towards or away from the eye.

A Cone of Rays

In about AD 1000 an Arab scientist, Alhazen, realized that we see an object because each part of it sends a ray of light into the eye. If you imagine looking at something round, like a saucer, the rays of light coming from its edges come together, or converge, as they get closer to the eye. The shape made by all the rays is like a cone, with its point at the eye. If the saucer is then moved closer to the eye, the cone of rays becomes shorter but wider, and so the saucer looks bigger. Despite the fact that Alhazen's idea was both simple and correct, it was ignored by most scientists for nearly 600 years.

Reflection, Refraction and Colour

People have known for thousands of years that light seems to travel in straight lines. Another early discovery was that when light hits a shiny surface it bounces off, or is reflected. When a ray of light strikes a flat mirror, the angle at which it reaches the mirror's surface (which is the angle of incidence) is the same as the angle at which it bounces off (the angle of reflection). If you look at something in a mirror, its image appears reversed left to right, and it also seems to be coming from behind the mirror.

When light rays pass into a transparent material, such as glass or water, they bend. This is called refraction. You can see it for yourself by putting a drinking straw into a glass of water. The light rays are refracted because glass and water are more dense than air, and the rays cannot travel through them as fast. When the rays enter the denser material they veer away from their normal path at an angle. They are refracted again when they emerge on the other side and pass back into the air.

Refraction is put to good use in lenses - pieces of glass or clear plastic with curved sides for spectacles, cameras, microscopes and other optical instruments. Lenses that bulge outwards are called convex lenses, and they bend light rays to make them converge at a point. The sides of a concave lens curve inwards, and they make light rays spread out.

A prism is a block of glass or clear plastic with ends that are triangular in shape. Since Aristotle's day, people have known that sunlight passing through a prism comes out in the form of a series of coloured rays. It was thought that the prism "stained" the light and made it coloured, but in 1666 Isaac Newton worked out what really happened inside the prism. He discovered that sunlight (so-called "white light") is actually made up of all the colours of the rainbow. When white light passes through a prism, the various colours are refracted at different angles and they spread out. Newton passed the coloured rays through a second prism and saw that they came together again as white light.

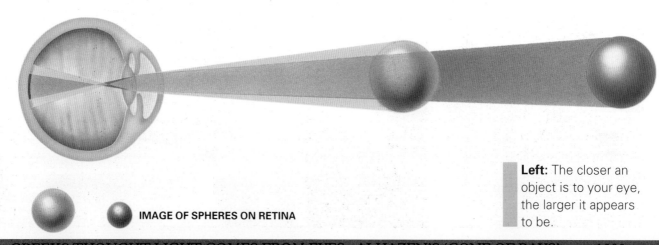

IMAGE OF SPHERES ON RETINA

Left: The closer an object is to your eye, the larger it appears to be.

LENSES

A convex lens focuses light rays to a point. A concave lens spreads out the rays. Both lenses refract light rays passing through them.

RAYS CONVERGE

LIGHT RAYS

FOCUS

CONVEX LENS

LIGHT RAYS

RAYS DIVERGE

CONCAVE LENS

Below: White light is refracted by these triangular glass prisms and split into its component colours.

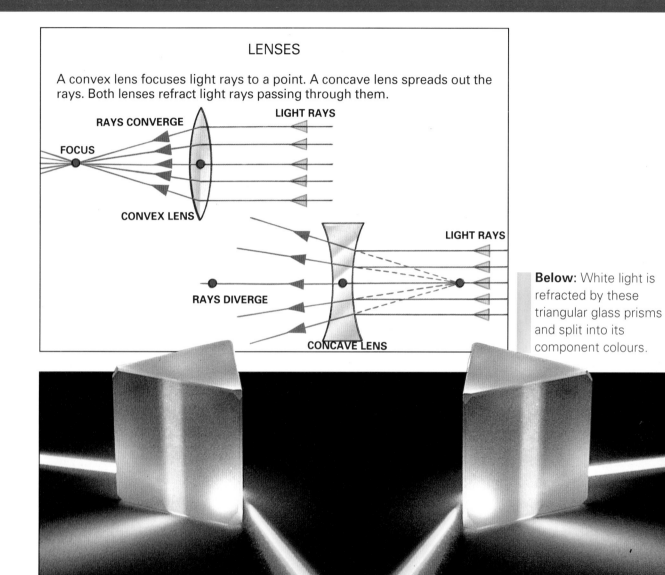

NEWTON'S PRISM EXPERIMENTS PROVE WHITE LIGHT IS MIXTURE OF COLOURS 1666

NATURE OF LIGHT

As well as trying to discover how light behaves, scientists have attempted for hundreds of years to find out what light actually is. In the 1660s Isaac Newton thought light consisted of tiny particles, which he called corpuscles. A few years later Christiaan Huygens, a Dutch physicist, suggested that light travels in waves, rather like the ripples which spread out when you drop a stone into a pond.

Young and Light Waves

Even though Huygens's theory could explain why reflection and refraction occurred, not many people were convinced that light waves existed. The person who proved Huygens correct was an Englishman named Thomas Young.

In 1801, Young performed an experiment in which light shone on to a screen through two narrow slits which were side by side. The source of the light was a sodium lamp, which produced light of a pure colour.

When Young looked at the screen, he saw alternating light and dark bands. He noticed that they looked rather like the ripples in a pond when two stones are thrown in at the same time next to each other. The ripples, or waves, combine so that where two waves meet they make a wave of double height, and where two troughs meet they make a trough twice as deep. This is called wave interference. Young realized that the bands on the screen were an interference pattern, which meant that light must consist of waves.

Each wave has a peak and a trough, and the distance between each two wave peaks is called the wavelength. Light of one colour has a different wavelength from that of another colour. Young chose a sodium light source because he knew it gave light of a pure colour; that is, light of a single wavelength. When he repeated his experiment using white light, the bands on the screen became a complicated pattern of colours. The light had

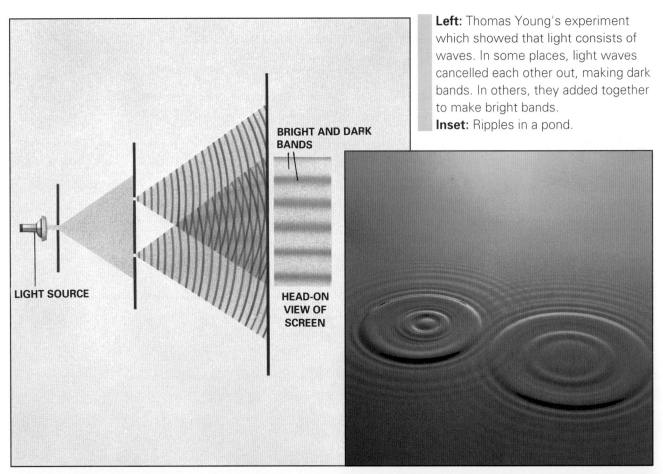

Left: Thomas Young's experiment which showed that light consists of waves. In some places, light waves cancelled each other out, making dark bands. In others, they added together to make bright bands.
Inset: Ripples in a pond.

BRIGHT AND DARK BANDS

LIGHT SOURCE

HEAD-ON VIEW OF SCREEN

NEWTON'S CORPUSCULAR THEORY OF LIGHT 1660s • YOUNG'S WAVE EXPERIMENTS 1801

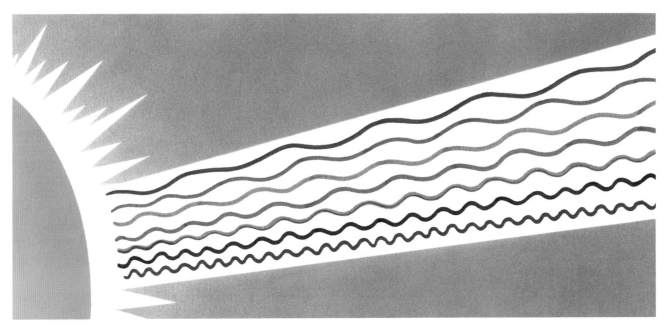

Left: Albert Einstein suggested that light is made of small packets of energy, called photons.

Above: White light consists of waves of coloured light with different wavelengths.

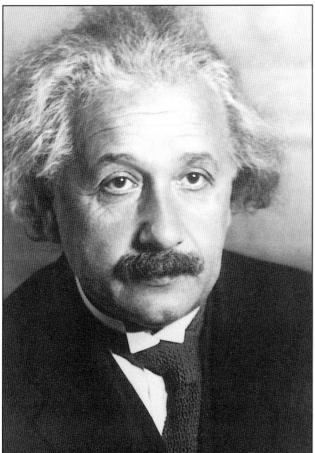

split into its different colours, making the interference pattern more difficult to interpret.

Einstein and Photons

In the early years of this century, the wave theory was modified by Albert Einstein. He suggested that light waves consist of small packets of energy, which were later named photons. In 1923 an American physicist called Compton found the first evidence that photons really do exist, and scientists today believe that light is made up of these particles travelling in waves. The way that light behaves depends upon certain circumstances. Sometimes it acts purely as a series of waves, but at other times the photons themselves seem more important and light will then behave as a stream of energy particles.

In his Theory of Relativity, Einstein predicted that nothing could travel faster than the speed of light. The first scientist to successfully measure the speed at which light travels in air was a Danish astronomer, Romer, who in 1676 calculated it to be 300,000 km per second.

EINSTEIN'S WAVES AND PHOTONS 1905 • COMPTON PROVES PHOTONS EXIST 1923

THE EYE

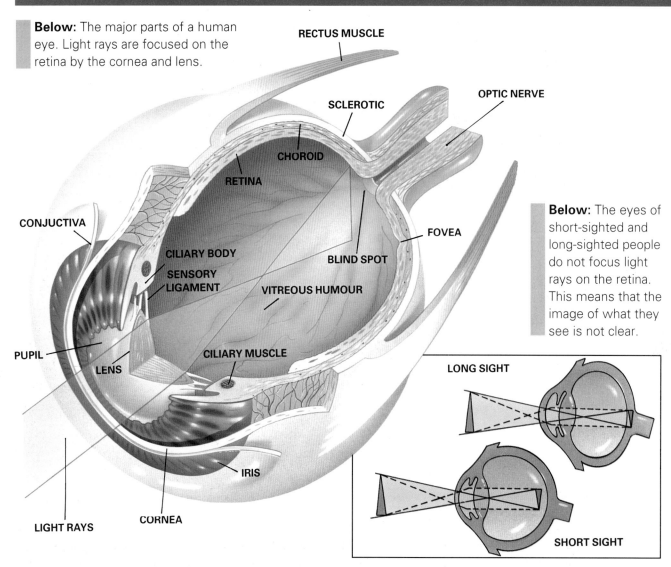

RECTUS MUSCLE

OPTIC NERVE

SCLEROTIC

CHOROID

RETINA

FOVEA

CONJUCTIVA

CILIARY BODY

BLIND SPOT

SENSORY LIGAMENT

VITREOUS HUMOUR

PUPIL

CILIARY MUSCLE

LENS

IRIS

LIGHT RAYS

CORNEA

LONG SIGHT

SHORT SIGHT

We gather information about the world around us by using our five senses: sight, hearing, smell, taste and touch. Of these, sight is by far the most important, and 80 per cent of the information stored in the brain comes from the eyes.

The Human Eye

Light entering the eye is focused by the cornea, a transparent disc at the front of the eye and by the lens behind it. They refract the light rays and make them converge. Around the outside of the lens are tiny muscles which expand and contract in order to change its shape and make the image of what we are looking at sharper. In between the cornea and the lens is a

coloured disc, the iris, with a hole in the middle, which is called the pupil. The pupil can be made larger to allow more light to enter the eye, or smaller to let through less light. In about 1850 the English surgeon Joseph Lister found that the iris was controlled by two separate sets of muscles, one set to make the pupil larger and the other to make it smaller.

When you look at something, the image of that object is focused on to the retina at the back of the eye, which consists of two types of minute cells, called rods and cones. Both are sensitive to light, although they work in different ways. Rods function in dim light and detect black and white, and cones only work in bright

Left and below: A photographic positive, made from the negative (below) where the natural colours are reversed.

light and detect colour. This is why it is difficult to see colours clearly at night.

There is a small, highly sensitive area on the retina called the fovea, which contains only cones, closely packed together. When you look closely at an object the image falls on the fovea to help you see most clearly.

The image formed on the retina is upside down and has to be turned the correct way up inside the brain. Information about the image is sent from the eye to the brain along the optic nerve at the back of the eye. There are no light-sensitive cells at the point where the optic nerve joins the retina, and so we can't see the part of an image that falls on this so-called blind spot.

The brain receives information from each of our eyes and puts it together to form a single "picture". As our eyes are several centimetres apart they each receive a slightly different view of an object, and this gives us the ability to see in three dimensions.

Cameras

A camera works in a very similar way to the eye. It has a lens which focuses the image of an object, and an aperture like the pupil which can be made larger or smaller to let in more or less light. In modern cameras the image is formed on a piece of transparent plastic coated with light-sensitive chemicals, but earlier ones used metal or glass plates instead of plastic film.

The first photograph ever taken was by a French soldier, Joseph Niépce, in 1816. He had to wait a whole day for the image to form because the light-sensitive chemicals he used were very slow to work. Soon after, another Frenchman, Louis Daguerre, invented a much more sensitive, faster process, which meant that people could be photographed for the first time.

An important breakthrough was made by the Englishman William Fox Talbot. He found a simple way of producing first a "negative" image, in which black areas of an object appear white, and white parts are black, and then making any number of "positive" pictures from the negative.

ELECTROMAGNETIC WAVES

The light that we can see is known as the visible spectrum. At one end of this spectrum is red light, which has the longest wavelength that our eyes can detect, and at the other end is violet light, which has the shortest wavelength we can see.

Out of Sight

Beyond each end of the visible spectrum are waves with wavelengths that cannot be detected by our eyes. Waves just beyond those of violet light are called ultraviolet; although their shorter wavelength makes them invisible to us, the eyes of bees are sensitive to ultraviolet waves. On the far side of the red end of the visible spectrum are longer waves, which are called infrared. They too are outside our range of vision, although special "thermographic" cameras can take infrared pictures.

Infrared is also called thermal radiation. Thermal means "to do with heat", and this gives us a clue that light is not the only thing that travels in waves. Beyond infrared are microwaves and, with an even longer wavelength, radio waves. On the other side of the visible spectrum, with progressively shorter wavelengths, are X-rays and gamma rays.

Maxwell and Electromagnetic Waves

All of the waves just mentioned are parts of what is called the electromagnetic spectrum. The link between electricity and magnetism was first discovered in 1819 by a Danish scientist, Hans Christian Oersted. Some years later, the Scottish physicist James Clerk Maxwell proved mathematically that light waves were a combination of electricity and magnetism. He called such waves electromagnetic waves. However, he could not prove his theory experimentally.

In 1889 a German physicist, Heinrich Hertz, produced radio waves and was able to show that they, too, are electromagnetic waves which differ from light waves only in that they have longer wavelengths. Since then, scientists have discovered that X-rays, gamma rays, infrared and microwaves are also electromagnetic waves. They are all part of what is called the electromagnetic spectrum, and they all travel at the speed of light. The visible light that we can see falls roughly in the middle of the electromagnetic spectrum.

Modern science has found uses for all types of electromagnetic waves. Gamma rays and X-rays are

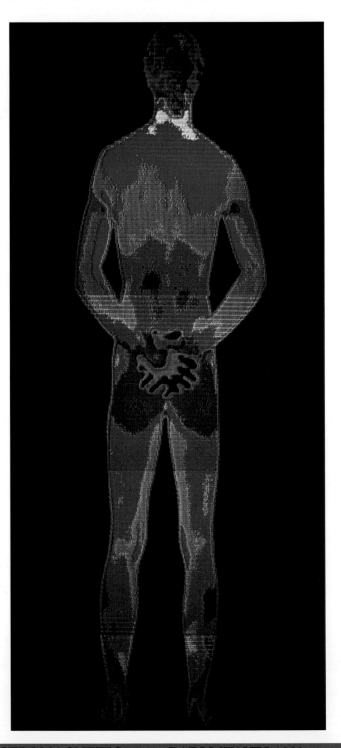

Below: A thermal image of a man. The hottest areas are white, and the coldest are dark blue or black.

The PHYSICAL WORLD

Below: The electromagnetic spectrum. The wavelength increases from left to right, while the frequency decreases.

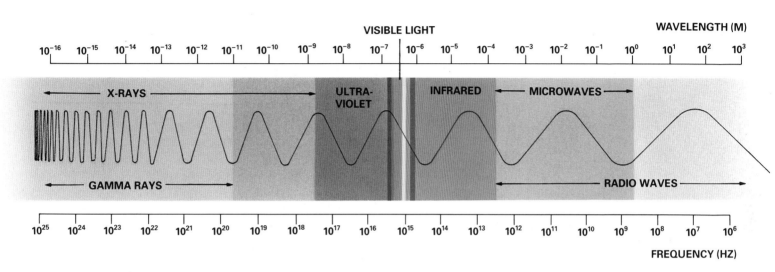

VISIBLE LIGHT

WAVELENGTH (M)

| 10^{-16} | 10^{-15} | 10^{-14} | 10^{-13} | 10^{-12} | 10^{-11} | 10^{-10} | 10^{-9} | 10^{-8} | 10^{-7} | 10^{-6} | 10^{-5} | 10^{-4} | 10^{-3} | 10^{-2} | 10^{-1} | 10^{0} | 10^{1} | 10^{2} | 10^{3} |

X-RAYS   ULTRA-VIOLET   INFRARED   MICROWAVES

GAMMA RAYS   RADIO WAVES

| 10^{25} | 10^{24} | 10^{23} | 10^{22} | 10^{21} | 10^{20} | 10^{19} | 10^{18} | 10^{17} | 10^{16} | 10^{15} | 10^{14} | 10^{13} | 10^{12} | 10^{11} | 10^{10} | 10^{9} | 10^{8} | 10^{7} | 10^{6} |

FREQUENCY (HZ)

used in medicine to kill cancer tumours in the body. They can be aimed very precisely at a tumour so that few healthy cells are damaged at the same time. X-rays are also used to take "pictures" of the body. They pass through the skin and tissues more easily than through bone, and so broken bones can be detected by placing the patient between an X-ray source and a metal screen that is sensitive to the rays. Microwaves can send telephone calls through the air and carry information to and from space satellites. They can also be used for cooking food. Radio waves are most commonly used to carry sound signals.

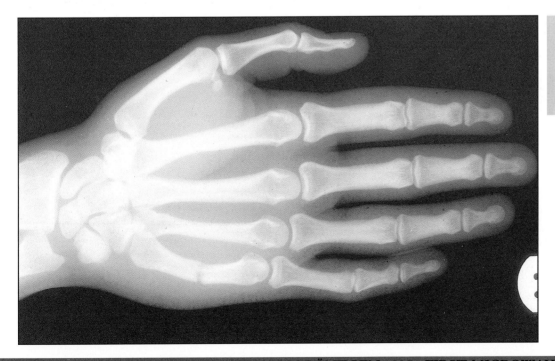

Left: An X-ray image of a human hand. The broken bone at the base of the little finger shows up clearly.

X-RAYS DISCOVERED BY WILHELM RÖNTGEN 1895 • FIRST MICROWAVE OVEN 1967

35

SOUND

There are quite a lot of similarities between sound and light. Both of them travel as waves, and can be reflected and refracted. However, they are produced in different ways and their waves are different, too.

Vibration and Sound Waves

Sounds are made when objects vibrate, or move quickly to and fro. If you pluck the string of a guitar or another stringed instrument you can see the string vibrate and hear the sound it makes. The sound of your voice is made by vocal chords inside your throat vibrating.

When an object vibrates it pushes the air molecules in front of it, bunching them up. The air molecules which are squashed together form a small area of high pressure. As the object moves back in the opposite direction, it leaves an area of low pressure where the air molecules are more spread out. These areas of high and low pressure move outwards from the vibrating object as sound waves.

This shows us that there is a very important differ-ence between light and sound. Light waves are electro-magnetic waves and they do not need air or any other "medium" to enable them to travel. Sound waves are vibration waves and they can only exist in a medium which has molecules that can be moved closer together and further apart. For example, as there is no air in outer space, there is no sound either; sometimes stars in far-away galaxies explode in complete silence.

Frequency, Amplitude and Speed

As in the case of light, the distance from the top of one sound wave to the next is called the wavelength. The number of complete sound waves or vibrations each second is called the frequency. The greater the fre-quency, the higher the pitch of the sound. Frequency is measured in hertz, named after Heinrich Hertz, the German physicist who experimented with radio waves in the late 1890s.

When the source of a sound is moving towards us it seems to have a higher pitch than when it is moving

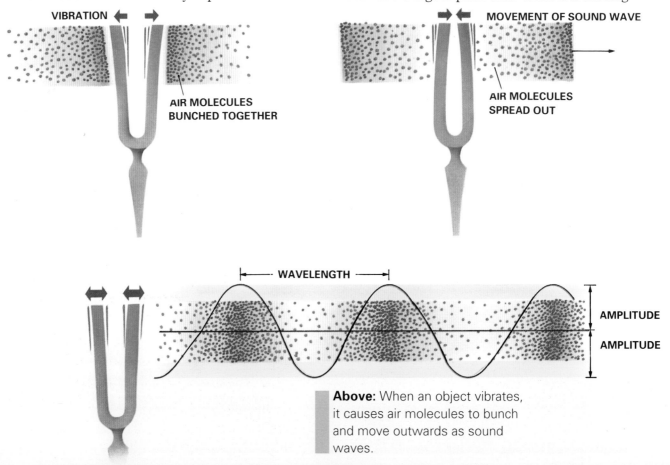

VIBRATION

AIR MOLECULES BUNCHED TOGETHER

MOVEMENT OF SOUND WAVE

AIR MOLECULES SPREAD OUT

WAVELENGTH

AMPLITUDE

AMPLITUDE

Above: When an object vibrates, it causes air molecules to bunch and move outwards as sound waves.

DOPPLER EFFECT OBSERVED BY CHRISTIAN DOPPLER 1845

away. This is called the Doppler effect, after Christian Doppler who discovered it in 1845. You can hear it for yourself if you listen to the siren of an ambulance or police car. It happens because the sound waves are squashed together as the siren approaches, making the frequency seem higher, and spread out more as the siren moves away.

The height of a sound wave is known as its amplitude. The larger the amplitude of a wave, the louder the sound. The loudness of sounds is measured in units called decibels.

The speed at which sound waves travel depends upon the medium through which they are moving. In air it is 332 metres per second, while in seawater it is nearly 1,500 metres per second. The speed of sound waves also increases as the temperature rises.

Sound waves can be reflected and refracted. They can also be diffracted, or bent around corners. Low-frequency sounds are diffracted more than higher ones.

Above: Part of Hertz's apparatus for studying waves.

Below: An example of the Doppler effect in action.

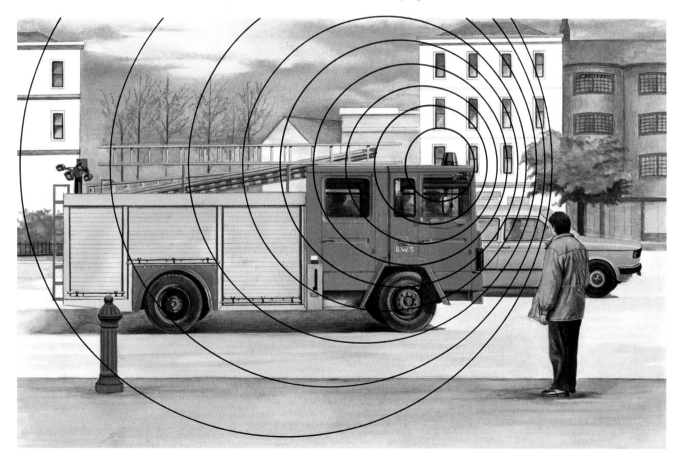

HEARING SOUND

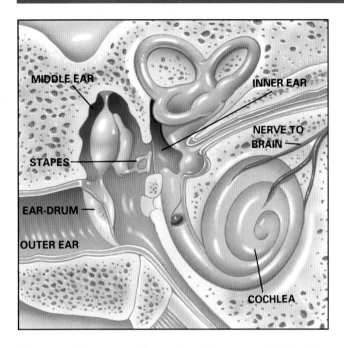

Humans, like many other animals, have ears for hearing sound. The flaps of skin on the sides of your head help to direct sound into a tube called the outer ear. At the end of this tube is the ear-drum, a thin, tightly stretched piece of skin which vibrates when sound waves reach it. The vibrations are passed on to the middle ear, which contains three small bones that act rather like levers and increase the force of the vibrations. The innermost bone, the stapes, pushes against another stretched piece of skin separating the middle ear from the inner ear. The inner ear is filled with fluid which is made to vibrate by the stapes, and the vibrations are picked up by thousands of sensitive hairs inside a coiled tube (the cochlea). The hairs then send signals to the brain which are interpreted as sounds.

What Can We Hear?

The softest sounds that human ears can detect are about as loud as the rustling of leaves. This sound has a loudness of just over 0 decibels. A normal conversation between two people is about 50 to 70 decibels, while the sound made by a jet aircraft is between 120 and 140 decibels. Sounds louder than 140 decibels can be painful and can damage our ears.

There are limits to the frequency of sound that our ears can hear. The lowest sound that most people can hear has a frequency of about 20 hertz. At the other end of the scale, the highest sound adults can hear is about 16,000 hertz; young people have more sensitive ears and can hear frequencies up to about 20,000 hertz.

Ultrasound and Infrasound

Just as there are types of electromagnetic radiation that our eyes cannot see, there are also sounds that our ears are unable to hear. Sound waves with frequencies greater than 20,000 hertz are called ultrasound. Although we cannot hear ultrasound, many animals can. Dogs, for example, can hear up to about 35,000 hertz, while rats and mice squeak to each other at frequencies up to 100,000 hertz.

Some creatures rely much more on their ears than on their eyes. Insect-eating bats can detect a tiny insect in the dark at a distance of more than 20 m by sending out ultrasound clicks which bounce back from the intended prey as echoes. The bat's highly sensitive ears pick up the echoes, and the time between sending out

Above left: The main parts of the human ear that enable us to hear sounds.

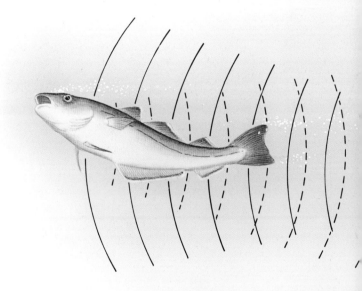

a click and hearing its echo tells the bat how far away the insect is. As it homes in on its prey, the bat speeds up its clicks to pinpoint the insect's position exactly.

Sound waves with frequencies lower than 20 hertz are known as infrasound. They can travel hundreds of kilometres. Tremors under the surface of the earth and waves at the seaside both produce infrasonic waves. Some very large creatures, such as elephants and whales, communicate with each other over long distances using infrasound.

Below: Dolphins use ultrasonic clicks to locate prey.

Right: An ultrasound image of a baby in its mother's womb.

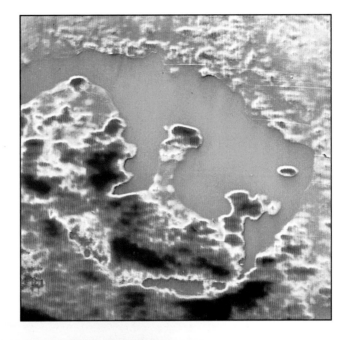

INFRASOUNDS HAVE FREQUENCIES UNDER 20 HZ • ULTRASOUND OVER 20,000 HZ

STATIC ELECTRICITY

Below: In 1752 Benjamin Franklin carried out an experiment in which he proved that lightning flashes are large electric sparks.

GREEKS DISCOVER ELECTRICITY c.600 BC • DU FAY FINDS TWO TYPES OF CHARGE 1734

Above: The Leyden jar, invented in 1745, was the first device for storing electrical charges.

The ancient Greeks discovered electricity more than 2,500 years ago. In 600 BC a scientist called Thales noticed that amber, a natural resin, attracted silk fibres when they were being spun. The word electricity comes from the Greek name for amber, elektron.

Gilbert and du Fay

Very little progress was made in the study of electricity until William Gilbert, an Englishman, found that other materials besides amber could be electrified. It was Gilbert who first used the word electricity. Although he was successful with glass, he could not electrify metals and he believed that was impossible. In 1734 he was proved wrong by the French scientist Charles du Fay. He found that metals could be electrified, but only if they were held in a handle made of glass or amber and not in the hand.

In his experiments, du Fay discovered another important fact: there are two kinds of electrification, which were later called positive and negative charges. A positive charge and a negative charge attract one another, while two charges that are the same push each other away. You can demonstrate this by rubbing an inflated balloon on a woollen sweater, which gives the balloon a negative charge. If you hold it up to a wall it will stay there, because its negative charges are attracted to the positive charges in the wall. If you negatively charge two balloons and hold them together they will push apart because they both have the same charge.

Between 1727 and 1729, Stephen Gray had found that electricity could flow freely through certain things, such as the human body and water. Other materials, such as glass and amber, would not allow electricity to flow through them. The French inventor Jean Desaguliers called materials through which electricity flows easily "conductors", and those through which it would not "insulators".

Storing Charge

In 1745 a device was invented in which electrical charges could be stored. Such things are now called capacitors. The Leyden jar, made by Petrus van Musschenbroek, became an object of curiosity throughout Europe and people travelled from far and wide to see how it produced electricity.

This development led Benjamin Franklin, an American scientist and inventor, to carry out a famous, and very dangerous, experiment in 1752. He tied a key to the string of a kite and flew the kite during a lightning storm. Electricity flowed down the string and made a spark on the key. By using lightning to charge a Leyden jar, Franklin proved that it was a large electric spark that carried electricity from thunderclouds to the ground. He later made a fortune selling his lightning conductor, a metal strip that runs from the top of a tall building to the ground and carries away electricity safely if the building is struck by lightning.

In 1785 Charles de Coulomb, a French physicist, was able to describe the basic laws of static electricity (electricity that stays in one place and does not move). One of these was that the force of attraction or repulsion between two charged objects depends upon the distance between them. The unit in which electric charge is measured is now called the coulomb in his honour.

ELECTRIC CURRENTS

When electricity moves through a conductor, we say that an electric current is flowing. A current moves along a wire rather like water flows through a pipe. Like the water, a current needs a force to push it along the wire. This electrical force can be provided by a battery.

Volta's Chemical Battery

The first battery was invented in 1799 by the Italian scientist Alessandro Volta. He made it from layers of silver, blotting paper soaked in sulphuric acid, and zinc. Electrical force, or potential difference as it is often known, is now measured in units called volts.

The size of the current that flows through a wire depends to some extent on the potential difference. A larger potential difference will produce a larger current. Electric currents are measured in units called amperes, after André Marie Ampère, the Frenchman who car-ried out early experiments on currents in the 1820s.

There is also another factor which affects the size of a current. Water slows down as it passes through a pipe (because of friction), and so does electric current flowing through a wire. The slowing down of a current is caused by resistance. It is measured in ohms, after Georg Simon Ohm who experimented with currents flowing through electric circuits. (The simplest electric circuit consists of a wire connected to a battery in an unbroken path.) In 1827 he discovered that the resistance of a wire equals the potential difference, or voltage, divided by the current. Known as Ohm's Law, this means that if a circuit has a high resistance, a large voltage is needed to make a current flow.

In 1841 James Prescott Joule, an English physicist, found that when a current flows through a wire, the wire

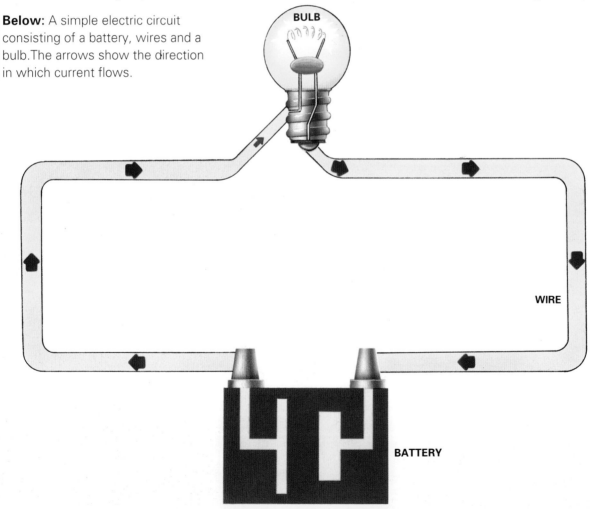

Below: A simple electric circuit consisting of a battery, wires and a bulb. The arrows show the direction in which current flows.

BULB

WIRE

BATTERY

heats up. This effect is caused by the resistance of the wire. The thinner the wire, the greater the resistance, and the greater the amount of heat produced. An electric light bulb contains very thin wire of high resistance which glows when it heats up. The fuse in an electric plug uses the Joule effect as a safety measure. It has a fixed resistance so that if too large a current flows through it the fuse melts (harmlessly inside an insulated casing) and breaks the circuit.

The type of current produced by a battery is called direct current, or DC. The electricity that we use in our homes, for such things as lights and electrical appliances like fridges and televisions, is of a different type, called alternating current, or AC. This type of current flows around a circuit first in one direction and then in the other.

The Origin of Electricity

By the mid-nineteenth century, scientists knew a great deal about how electricity behaves, but they did not know where it came from. In 1875 Joseph John Thomson discovered that atoms contain particles called electrons. Each electron has a tiny negative charge, and it is the movement of electrons that produces electricity.

When a balloon is rubbed on wool, it becomes negatively charged because electrons are transferred from the wool to the balloon. An electric current flowing along a wire is actually a stream of electrons moving from the negative terminal of a battery towards the positive terminal. Resistance occurs because the electrons sometimes collide with the metal atoms in the wire. These collisions produce the heat that Joule noticed in 1841.

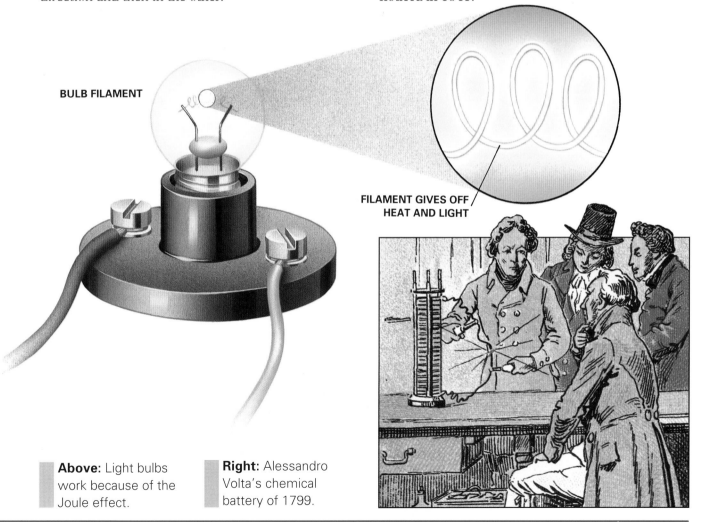

BULB FILAMENT

FILAMENT GIVES OFF HEAT AND LIGHT

Above: Light bulbs work because of the Joule effect.

Right: Alessandro Volta's chemical battery of 1799.

MAGNETISM

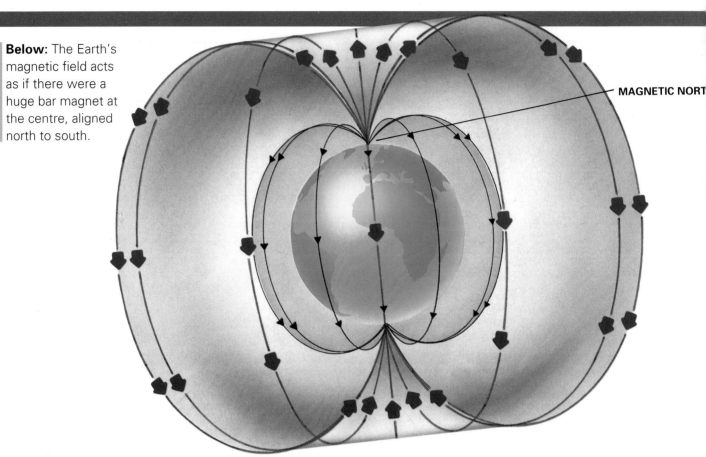

Below: The Earth's magnetic field acts as if there were a huge bar magnet at the centre, aligned north to south.

MAGNETIC NORTH

As is the case in many other areas of science, the ancient Greeks knew about magnetism 2,500 years ago. They discovered rocks which could pick up small pieces of iron, such as nails.

Magnets and Fields

Magnets attract objects made of iron, steel and some other metals. However, most metals, including copper, aluminium and gold, are non-magnetic, and so are cloth, paper, glass and plastic.

Not all parts of a magnet are equally magnetic; the strongest points are usually near to the ends of a magnet, and are called the north pole and south pole. In the thirteenth century a scientist called Peter Peregrinus found that the north pole of one magnet attracts the south pole of another, while two north poles (or two south poles) repel each other.

The area around a magnet in which magnetism can be detected is called a magnetic field. The field is strongest near the poles and gets weaker further away from them. In the sixteenth century the Englishman William Gilbert realized that the Earth itself is an

enormous magnet, with a north and a south pole. These magnetic poles are not in the same place as the geographic North Pole and South Pole.

If a magnet is able to move freely, it will turn in order to line itself up with the Earth's field, so that one end, the north pole, points towards the north, and the south pole points south. A compass consists of a magnetic needle which points north and helps navigators in ships and aircraft to know the direction in which they are travelling. The Earth's magnetic field can also be detected 80,000 km into space.

You can magnetize a steel needle by stroking it with a magnet. This is possible because the atoms inside a magnetic material, like steel, are all tiny magnets themselves. When the needle is stroked with the magnet all of the atoms line up to point in the same direction, with their north poles facing one way and their south poles facing the other.

Electricity and Magnetism

In 1819 Hans Christian Oersted discovered that an electric current flowing through a wire moved the

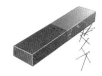

needle of a nearby compass. The current had produced a magnetic field around the wire. This phenomenon is known as electromagnetism. The strength of a field produced in this way depends upon the size of the current, the length of the wire and the distance from the wire.

The first electromagnet was made in 1820 by François Arago. He coiled copper wire around an iron bar and passed a current through it. The coil produced a magnetic field which magnetized the iron bar. The strength of an electromagnetic field increases if the current passed through the coil is made larger, and if the number of turns of wire in the coil is increased.

Following the work of Oersted, Arago and others, Michael Faraday tried to do the reverse of what they had achieved: produce an electric current using a magnetic field, known as electromagnetic induction. He struggled with the problem for 6 years, and finally succeeded in 1831. Faraday's achievement led to the development of generators, which produce electricity from the movement of a wire through a magnetic field. An electric motor works in the opposite way: an electric current flowing through a wire in a magnetic field causes the wire to move.

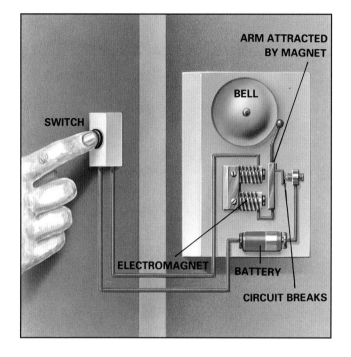

Above: An electric bell uses an electro-magnet.

Below: Michael Faraday at work in his laboratory.

ARAGO'S ELECTROMAGNET 1820 • FARADAY'S ELECTROMAGNETIC INDUCTION 1831

COMPUTERS

Computers are machines designed to store, recall and process information. The effectiveness or power of a computer is usually measured in terms of the amount of information it can store in its memory, and the number of instructions it can carry out per second.

The First Computers

The origins of the computer date back 5,000 years to the invention of the abacus. During the seventeenth century mechanical calculating machines were devised by Blaise Pascal, Gottfried von Liebnitz and others, but one of the most important advances came from an unlikely direction, silk weaving machines. In 1805 the Frenchman Joseph-Marie Jacquard invented a loom which could be programmed to weave different patterns by inserting one of a number of cards with holes punched in various positions. Thirty years later, Charles Babbage designed what he called the Analytical Engine, a calculating machine into which information was inserted by means of punched cards.

In 1886 Hermann Hollerich combined the advances made by Jacquard and Babbage with new electromagnetic inventions to produce a machine which could sort information into different categories. An American, George Stibitz, invented the first binary computer in 1939. Binary means "two", and in the binary system only two digits (1 and 0) are used to express numbers. In binary computers, the digit 1 means that an electric current flows and 0 means that no current flows. All modern computers use the binary system.

The world's first successful computer, called ENIAC (Electronic Numerical Integrator and Calculator), was built in 1946. It contained over 18,000 switches called valves, and filled a large room. Two years later came UNIVAC (Universal Automatic Computer), the first machine to be programmed with information on magnetic tape instead of punched tape or cards.

Semiconductors and Silicon Chips

When you think of a modern computer, you probably think of a small machine that fits quite neatly on top of a desk. Despite its size, a desktop computer may contain hundreds of thousands of electronic parts. How do they all fit inside?

Until fairly recently, the electronic components from which computers were made were all quite large

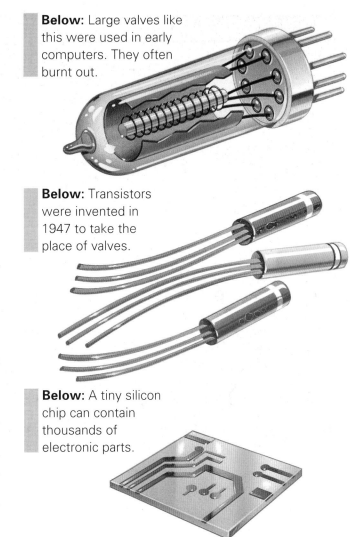

Below: Large valves like this were used in early computers. They often burnt out.

Below: Transistors were invented in 1947 to take the place of valves.

Below: A tiny silicon chip can contain thousands of electronic parts.

and bulky. The first step towards building smaller computers came with the use of materials known as semiconductors. Normally, semiconductors do not conduct electricity, but under certain conditions they allow a very small electric current to flow. In 1947 William Shockley, John Bardeen and Walter Brattain found a way of using semiconductors to make a new type of switch, the transistor. Transistors are only a fraction of the size of valves, and their invention revolutionized computers. Even so, computers of the 1950s were much larger and less powerful than those of today.

Then, in 1958, an American company, Texas Instruments, developed the integrated circuit. This consisted of a thin slice of silicon (a semiconductor) on

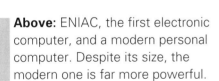

Above: ENIAC, the first electronic computer, and a modern personal computer. Despite its size, the modern one is far more powerful.

Below: A magnified view of a modern silicon chip, showing the vast number of electronic components it contains.

which were placed a variety of electronic components, including transistors, all connected with tiny threads of metal. Integrated circuits soon became known as silicon chips, microchips or, simply, chips.

Since then, it has become possible to put more and more components on a chip. Several thousand components can now be fitted on to a chip no bigger than a fingernail. In 1990 one manufacturer produced a chip, 14 cm square, with 4 million transistors crammed on to its surface.

The largest modern computers, called supercomputers, are staggeringly powerful. One of these, the Cray-2, contains over 200,000 silicon chips and can carry out several billion calculations every second.

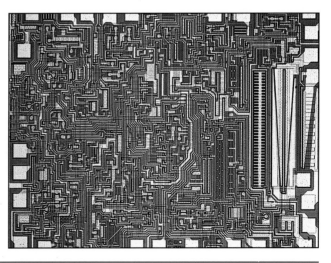

ENIAC COMPUTER 1946 • TRANSISTOR INVENTED 1947 • FIRST INTEGRATED CIRCUIT 1958

RADIOACTIVITY

Not all scientific discoveries are made as a result of scientists working to solve a particular problem; some happen by pure chance. One of the most famous "accidental" discoveries was that of radioactivity.

Becquerel and the Curies

One day in 1896, the Frenchman Henri Becquerel began an experiment. He wanted to see if a substance containing uranium gave off X-rays (which had been discovered the previous year) when exposed to sunlight. He could not finish the experiment because the weather was too cloudy, and he put away his equipment. A few days later he tried again, and placed the uranium samples on a photographic plate that had not been taken out of its wrapping. Later, when he developed the plate, he was surprised to see an image that matched the shapes of the samples. He concluded that the uranium was giving off rays, which he called

radiation, that affected the photographic plate but he did not understand how the radiation was produced.

Becquerel took the problem to his friends, Pierre and Marie Curie. They spent 2 years examining pitchblende (the ore from which uranium comes) and, in 1898, found that it contained two previously unknown elements, which were given the names radium and polonium. Both of these elements gave off radiation much more strongly than uranium.

In 1899 Ernest Rutherford found that uranium gave off two types of radiation, which he call alpha and beta rays. A third type, gamma rays, was discovered in 1900. Two years later the English physicist Frederick Soddy was able to explain how radioactivity was produced. He showed that the nuclei of some atoms are unstable and, as a result, they break up and give off energy in the form of radiation.

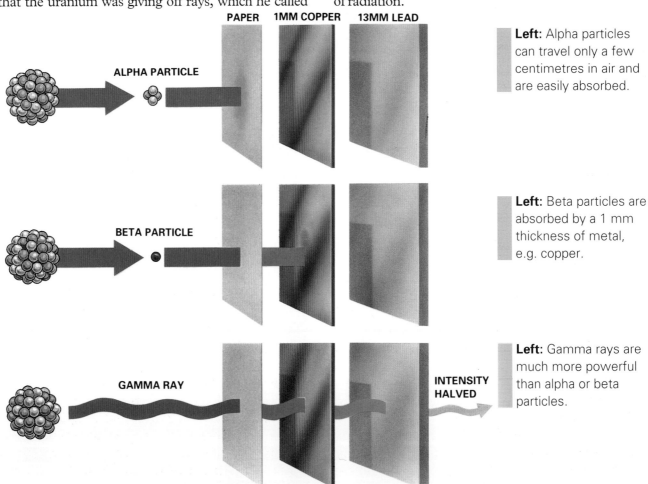

PAPER **1MM COPPER** **13MM LEAD**

ALPHA PARTICLE

Left: Alpha particles can travel only a few centimetres in air and are easily absorbed.

BETA PARTICLE

Left: Beta particles are absorbed by a 1 mm thickness of metal, e.g. copper.

GAMMA RAY

INTENSITY HALVED

Left: Gamma rays are much more powerful than alpha or beta particles.

THE PHYSICAL WORLD

URANIUM-238 (RADIOACTIVE)

2 STAGES

BETA PARTICLE (ELECTRON)

ALPHA PARTICLE

PROTACTINIUM-234

7 STAGES

BISMUTH-214

ALPHA PARTICLE

LEAD-206 (STABLE)

4 STAGES

BETA PARTICLE

POLONIUM-214

Below: Radioactive atoms break down by giving off alpha or beta particles and changing into other atoms. Radioactive uranium-238 breaks down into stable lead-206 in about 14 stages.

Below: Marie and Pierre Curie discovered several radioactive elements.

The atoms of a particular element all have the same number of protons in their nuclei, but some may have more neutrons than others. Atoms of one element which have different numbers of neutrons are called isotopes, and almost all elements have several such isotopes. Many isotopes are quite stable and do not change. Others are unstable and as their nuclei break up, or decay, they give off radiation. (This is just as Soddy suggested, although he did not know what caused instability in the nucleus as neutrons were not discovered until 1932.)

In 1934 the Curie family made another breakthrough. All of the work on radioactivity had been carried out using radioactive elements that occur naturally. Irène and Frédéric Joliot-Curie (daughter and son-in-law of Pierre and Marie) made an "artificially" radioactive isotope by bombarding aluminium with alpha particles. Their success has led to the production of many other new radioactive isotopes which are used in biology, medicine and other scientific fields.

Half-life and Radiocarbon Dating

Different radioactive isotopes break down at different rates. The speed at which they break down is measured in terms of what is called half-life. This is the time it takes for half of the nuclei in a radioactive sample to decay. Some isotopes have half-lives of a fraction of a second, while others are much longer.

An isotope of carbon, called carbon-14, has a half-life of 5,730 years. As carbon is one of the most common elements found on earth, the decay of its radioactive isotope has given us a method of telling how old some materials are. By measuring the amount of carbon-14 still present in the material, and knowing the half-life, scientists can calculate its age.

ALPHA, BETA AND GAMMA RADIATION 1899-1900 • ARTIFICIAL RADIOACTIVITY 1934

FISSION AND FUSION

The nucleus at the centre of an atom contains huge amounts of energy. This energy can be released in what are called nuclear reactions.

Nuclear Fission

Fission is a nuclear reaction in which a heavy, unstable nucleus is split into two or more lighter nuclei. In the process, a number of neutrons are given off.

Sometimes fission occurs naturally, but in the main it is made to happen by artificial methods. Not all nuclei can be made to fission; those which can, such as the isotopes plutonium-239 and uranium-235, are described as being fissile.

The most common method of producing fission is to fire a particle, such as a neutron, at a heavy nucleus. When the nucleus absorbs the neutron it becomes unstable and fissions. It gives out neutrons and energy in the form of heat. If there are other heavy nuclei present, they may be hit by the neutrons, causing more fissions, and so on. This is called a chain reaction. The minimum amount of material which needs to be present for a chain reaction to happen is known as the critical mass. The first so-called atomic pile in which fission was produced was made in the USA in 1942, by the Italian scientist Enrico Fermi.

Nuclear fission is most commonly used in nuclear power stations. The fuel used in the reactors of most nuclear power stations is in the form of rods containing uranium, some of which is uranium-235 and some uranium-238. The most reactive of these is uranium-235. When its nucleus absorbs a neutron, it breaks down into isotopes of lanthanum and bromine, and gives off three neutrons and some heat. The chain reaction that takes place inside the reactor can be controlled by inserting or withdrawing fuel rods. The heat produced is used to turn water to steam, which turns turbines to produce electricity.

The first nuclear power station to produce electricity was built in the USA in 1951. A major drawback to the use of nuclear power stations is that the isotopes produced during fission are highly radioactive, and dangerous to living things.

The other use of fission is much more dangerous:

Below: In nuclear fission, a nucleus absorbs a neutron fired at it, becomes unstable, and breaks down to give off energy as heat.

Below: In nuclear fusion, two light nuclei are forced to combine into a single heavy one. Large amounts of energy are released.

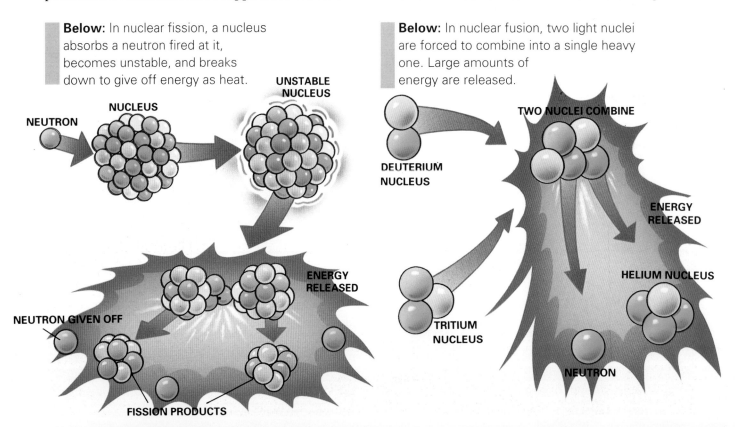

NEUTRON   NUCLEUS   UNSTABLE NUCLEUS

ENERGY RELEASED

NEUTRON GIVEN OFF

FISSION PRODUCTS

TWO NUCLEI COMBINE

DEUTERIUM NUCLEUS

ENERGY RELEASED

HELIUM NUCLEUS

TRITIUM NUCLEUS

NEUTRON

nuclear weapons. Although the fission process is the same inside both a reactor and a nuclear bomb, the chain reaction in a bomb is not controlled and so it causes an explosion and a massive release of energy.

Nuclear Fusion

Fusion occurs in a different way from fission. Instead of heavy nuclei breaking down into lighter ones, two light nuclei are made to collide and join together to make a single heavy one. An example of a fusion reaction is that between deuterium and tritium (two isotopes of hydrogen) which, on collision, produce helium, a single neutron and energy.

Nuclear fusion can only occur at extremely high temperatures, measured in millions of degrees Celsius. For this reason, fusion happens naturally only inside the sun and other stars. Uncontrolled fusion reactions have been carried out in the form of hydrogen bombs, but fusion cannot yet be put to more peaceful purposes. Scientists are trying to devise ways of building a fusion reactor. However, the problems of containing fuel at such high temperatures are, at present, impossible to solve. If the scientists succeed, the world's energy problems could be solved. What is more, unlike fission, fusion does not produce radioactive waste.

Below: A nuclear bomb is an example of an uncontrolled fission reaction. Huge amounts of energy are released by the explosion.

EARLY DISCOVERIES

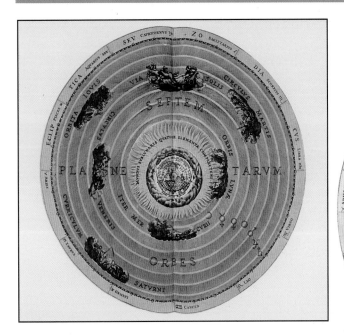

Above: Aristotle believed that the Earth was at the centre of the Universe.

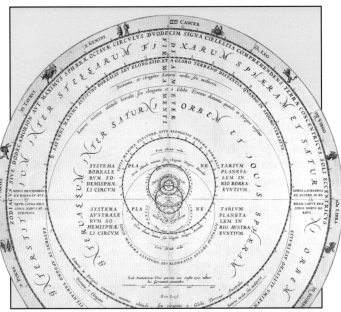

Above: Like Aristotle, Tycho Brahe thought the Earth was stationary at the centre of the Universe.

Aristotle, the ancient Greek philosopher, was one of the first people to have a definite idea about what the universe looks like, how the stars and planets are arranged and the way in which they move. Like almost everyone else at his time, Aristotle believed that the Earth was at the centre of the Universe and that the Sun, the Moon and the planets all orbited around it. Claudius Ptolemy, an astronomer who lived during the second century AD, revised Aristotle's ideas slightly and made very complicated calculations of the planets' orbits, but he still kept the Earth at the centre.

Copernicus and Galileo

This Earth-centred view of the Universe was not seriously challenged until the sixteenth century. In 1543 the astronomer Nicolaus Copernicus claimed that the Sun, not the Earth, was at the centre and that the Moon and planets all revolved around it. However, he had no real evidence for his belief. Like most other astronomers the Dane, Tycho Brahe, rejected Copernicus's theory; he thought it was impossible for the Earth to be moving around the Sun. He came up with his own idea of the Universe, again placing the Earth at

the centre. But his work did bring some progress. Comets and supernovae (exploding stars) had always been thought to be part of the Earth's weather system, but Tycho's observations showed him that they were much further out in space. Aristotle's theory received its first dent, but there was still no proof to support Copernicus. That was to come over 60 years later, following the invention of the telescope.

When he first learned of the invention, the Italian scientist Galileo quickly made a telescope of his own. His first version could magnify only nine times, but he immediately made an improved one with a magnification of thirty times. In 1609 he turned his telescope on the night sky.

What he saw amazed and delighted him. According to Aristotle, the Moon and the planets were all perfect spheres, but through his telescope Galileo saw that the Moon was covered with mountains and craters. When he looked at the planet Jupiter he found it has four moons, which disproved Aristotle's claim that only the Earth had a moon. These and other discoveries convinced Galileo that Copernicus was right.

COPERNICUS' SUN-CENTRED UNIVERSE 1543 • GALILEO'S TELESCOPE DISCOVERIES 1609

Above: Copernicus' view of the Universe had the Sun at the centre and the planets spinning around it.

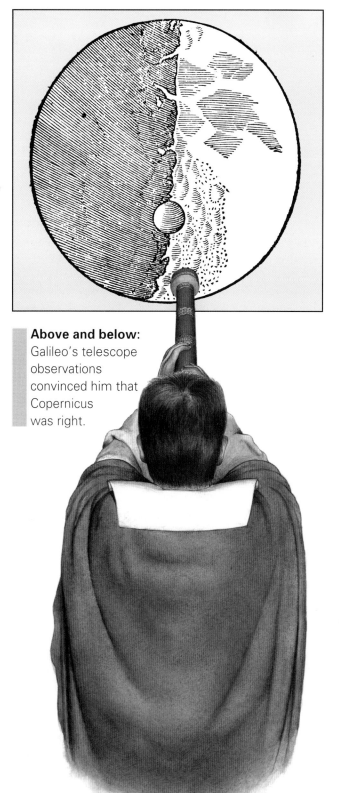

Above and below: Galileo's telescope observations convinced him that Copernicus was right.

Kepler and Newton

As astronomers came to accept the idea of a Sun-centred Universe, they turned their minds to the question of what held the planets in their orbits. In the early seventeenth century an astronomer called Johannes Kepler thought they might be held in place by a force radiating outwards from the Sun. In trying to prove this theory he made another important discovery, the orbits of the planets are not circular, but elliptical, rather like flattened circles. He also found a relationship between the time a planet takes to orbit the Sun and its distance from it: a planet twice as far away than another planet from the Sun will take four times as long to orbit it.

The question of what holds the planets in their orbits was finally solved by Isaac Newton. He invented a new telescope, called the reflecting telescope, which gave him a better view of the planets' motion. However, he used mathematics to make his most important discovery, that everything in the Universe is attracted to everything else by a force called gravity. The force of gravity between two objects depends upon their masses and how far apart they are (pp. 12-13).

KEPLER FINDS PLANETARY ORBITS ARE ELLIPTICAL 1610

MODERN ASTRONOMY

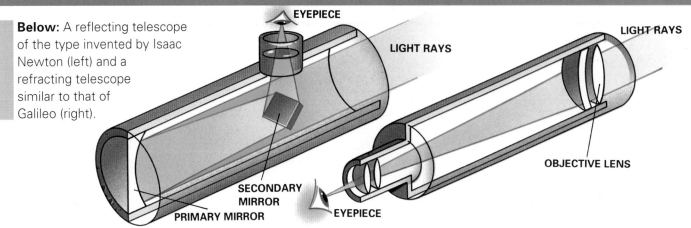

Below: A reflecting telescope of the type invented by Isaac Newton (left) and a refracting telescope similar to that of Galileo (right).

EYEPIECE

LIGHT RAYS

LIGHT RAYS

OBJECTIVE LENS

SECONDARY MIRROR

PRIMARY MIRROR

EYEPIECE

Although people have been watching the Sun, the Moon and the stars for thousands of years, great advances in the science of astronomy only began with the invention of the telescope. The earliest type, the refracting telescope used by Galileo, was little more than a tube with a lens at each end. Because it was then impossible to make very accurate lenses, early refracting telescopes could not be used to view planets further away than Saturn. Newton's reflecting telescope, in which light rays are bounced off mirrors, was an improvement and many of the world's astronomical observatories still use telescopes of this type. The largest reflector, with a 6 m mirror, is at Zelenchukskaya in Russia.

However, telescopes that rely on light cannot be used to see objects far out in space, because dust and moisture in the Earth's atmosphere stop some light passing through or scatter it in all directions. Astrono-

Right: The Hubble Space Telescope was launched from the Space Shuttle in April 1990. It was hoped that being outside the Earth's atmosphere would enable the telescope to provide good images of space. But, after launching, it was found that its light-gathering mirrors were defective.

KARL JANSKY INVENTS RADIO TELESCOPE 1932 • RADAR ASTRONOMY FIRST USED 1946

mers try to reduce this problem by building observatories on the top of mountains, where the air is clear and dry, but this is not a complete solution.

Radioastronomy

Many recent discoveries have been made using instruments very different from normal, optical, telescopes. As well as light, stars give off other forms of electromagnetic radiation, including X-rays, gamma rays, ultraviolet rays, infrared rays and radio waves. The Earth's atmosphere blocks out or weakens most of these, however, and only radio waves can pass through freely.

Radio waves from stars were first detected in 1931, and the first radio telescope was built the following year by Karl Jansky. A radio telescope collects radio waves by means of long arrangements of wire aerials, or large dishes which can be moved to point at different parts of the sky. When the radio waves are received, they are first amplified (made stronger) and then fed into computers which convert them into visible images.

Some radio telescopes have a number of dishes which can all be moved into different positions. The array of small dishes gives the same results as one extremely large one would do. One of the largest radio telescopes of this type, with 27 dishes each measuring 26 m across, is the Very Large Array (VLA) at Socorro, New Mexico, in the USA. It is equivalent to a single dish 27 km in diameter.

Radio telescopes are sometimes designed to do more than just receive radio waves; for example, the largest radio dish in the world, at Arecibo, Puerto Rico, sends out radio signals aimed at nearby planets and then collects the waves that bounce back. Using this technique, called radar astronomy, scientists can produce images of a planet's surface. This has proved especially useful in the case of Venus, for example, the surface of which is hidden beneath layers of cloud and cannot be seen through normal optical telescopes.

Space Telecopes

During the 1960s, when the USA and USSR began sending more and more rockets into space, satellites containing scientific instruments, including telescopes and devices called detectors, were placed in orbit around the Earth. Because they are outside the Earth's atmosphere, these instruments can collect X-rays, gamma rays and other forms of electromagnetic radiation. They have provided astronomers with a vast amount of information about the universe, what it consists of, and how it began.

Below: The radiotelescope in Arecibo, Puerto Rico. Its antenna reflector consists of almost 39,000 sheets of aluminium mesh.

THE UNIVERSE

For many hundreds of years it was believed that the Earth was the centre of the Universe, and that everything else revolved around it. Modern astronomical discoveries have shown us that, in fact, our planet is no more than a tiny speck in the vast Universe.

The Earth, the Moon and the planets are all part of what is called the Solar System. At the centre is a star which we call the Sun. The Solar System is part of a whole cluster of stars, a galaxy, which is known as the

Milky Way. All the stars we can see in the night sky belong to the Milky Way. Throughout the Universe as a whole, there may be 100 billion galaxies, each containing billions of stars. It is quite likely that some of these stars have planets spinning around them, but none have yet been discovered.

The distances in space are so huge that they are measured in light years. One light year is the distance that light travels in a year, 9,465,000,000,000 km. The most distant objects in the Universe that astronomers have so far been able to observe are about 13,000 million light years away.

White Dwarfs and Red Giants

Not all stars look the same as our Sun. Some are smaller and others much, much larger. Stars do not live forever. Near the end of their life, some stars expand to form what are called red giants and then collapse in on themselves to become white dwarfs. Very large stars may live for only a few million years, at the end of which they explode and blow themselves apart, throwing out huge quantities of gas and dust.

In 1967 Jocelyn Bell discovered radio waves in the form of pulses coming from one such exploded star, or supernova. Astronomers have now identified more than 300 of these "pulsars", which are thought to be the collapsed centres of supernovae.

Some of the most fascinating objects to have been discovered are called quasars. When they were first noticed, in 1961, it was thought they were very small galaxies, but they give off hundreds of times more light than ordinary galaxies. It now seems that they might be eruptions taking place inside vast galaxies far away in

ASTRONOMY

space, so far that the galaxies themselves are invisible to us. One theory is that quasars get their immense power from black holes.

Black holes are thought to form when enormous stars collapse. They are small regions, perhaps less than 20 km across, of enormous gravity which swallow up matter around them. Evidence for the existence of black holes was first found by X-ray detectors carried aboard space satellites.

The Expanding Universe

Scientists now know that the Universe is expanding all the time, spreading outwards in all directions. This means that in the past it must have been smaller, and so there was probably a time when all the matter in what is now the Universe was packed in one place. It is thought that the Universe began with a huge explosion, called the Big Bang, about 15,000 million years ago, and that it has been expanding ever since. No one knows what will happen to the Universe in the distant future. It may just carry on expanding until all of the stars die out. Another theory is that it will eventually collapse in on itself and end in a Big Crunch.

Above: All the stars we can see in the night sky belong to our galaxy, the Milky Way. The galaxy is 100,000 light years across and contains 100,000 million stars. There may be as many as 100 billion other galaxies throughout the Universe.

Right: Our Solar System, containing the Sun, the Earth and other planets, is just a tiny part of the Milky Way.

BLACK HOLES FORMED FROM COLLAPSED STARS • BIG BANG 15,000 MILLION YEARS AGO

57

ELEMENTS

Everything in the Universe consists of combinations of substances called elements. The ancient Greeks believed that things on Earth were made of just four elements, earth, air, fire and water, while the rest of the Universe consisted of a fifth element, ether.

Scientists have discovered that in fact there are 92 elements which occur naturally on Earth, and they are not at all like those of the Greeks. Of these 92 "native" elements, only two, bromine and mercury, are liquids at normal temperature, 11 are gases and the rest are all solids. Most of the solids are metals.

One of the first elements to be identified was gold. This is because it appears in pure lumps, called nuggets. Many other elements do not occur in such a convenient form, but in combinations of elements known as compounds (pp. 60-1). Most such elements have been found by breaking down compounds. Silicon, which occurs in sand and other substances, is the second most common element on Earth after oxygen. It was first made in its pure form in 1823 by Jöns Jakob Berzelius.

Aluminium occurs in an ore called bauxite, in which it is combined with oxygen. The Danish scientist Hans Christian Oersted succeeded in separating out aluminium in 1825.

In recent years, scientists have made 18 new elements artificially, taking the total number up to 110. All of the new elements are radioactive, and most have been created using particle accelerators. Experiments are now underway to make the 111th element.

Elements and Atoms

We now know that an element is a substance which is made up of just one kind of atom. The element iron, for example, contains only iron atoms, which are different from the atoms of all other elements. This means that elements cannot be broken down into other, simpler substances.

What makes an atom of one element different from that of another is the number of protons inside the nucleus. This is called the atomic number. Hydrogen has a single proton, so its atomic number is 1; iron has

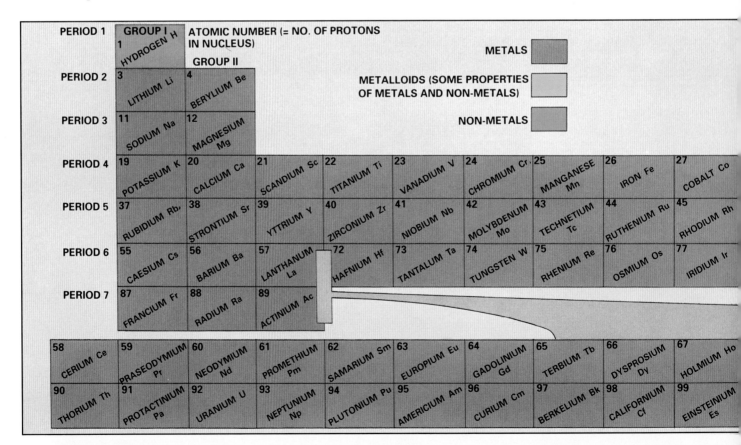

MATTER MADE OF 92 ELEMENTS & THEIR COMPOUNDS WITH 18 MAN-MADE ELEMENTS

26 protons and an atomic number of 26.

The Periodic Table

One of the most important developments in modern science was the drawing up of the Periodic Table of Elements. This was the work of a Russian scientist, Dmitri Mendeleev, in 1869. The illustration on this page shows a modern version of the table. Elements are arranged according to their atomic number, and each has a chemical symbol; the symbol for hydrogen is H, while that of gold is Au.

The vertical columns, or "groups", contain elements that have similar properties. The group on the right-hand side, for example, contains helium, neon, argon, krypton, xenon and radon, all of which are gases that do not combine, or "react", easily with other elements to form compounds. As you move to the left along a horizontal row, or "period", the elements become steadily more reactive, and those in the left-hand group are the most reactive of all. How reactive an element is depends on the way in which the electrons are arranged in its atoms.

Below: A modern version of the Periodic Table.

Right: New elements can be made using particle accelerators.

			GROUP III	GROUP IV	GROUP V	GROUP VI	GROUP VII	GROUP VIII 2 HELIUM He
			5 BORON B	6 CARBON C	7 NITROGEN N	8 OXYGEN O	9 FLUORINE F	10 NEON Ne
			13 ALUMINIUM Al	14 SILICON Si	15 PHOSPHORUS P	16 SULPHUR S	17 CHLORINE Cl	18 ARGON Ar
28 NICKEL Ni	29 COPPER Cu	30 ZINC Zn	31 GALLIUM Ga	32 GERMANIUM Ge	33 ARSENIC As	34 SELENIUM Se	35 BROMINE Br	36 KRYPTON Kr
46 PALLADIUM Pd	47 SILVER Ag	48 CADMIUM Cd	49 INDIUM In	50 TIN Sn	51 ANTIMONY Sb	52 TELLURIUM Te	53 IODINE I	54 XENON Xe
78 PLATINUM Pt	79 GOLD Au	80 MERCURY Hg	81 THALLIUM Tl	82 LEAD Pb	83 BISMUTH Bi	84 POLONIUM Po	85 ASTATINE At	86 RADON Rn

68 ERBIUM Er	69 THULIUM Tm	70 YTTERBIUM Yb	71 LUTETIUM Lu					
100 FERMIUM Fm	101 MENDELEVIUM Md	102 NOBELIUM No	103 LAWRENCIUM Lw	104 UNNILQUADIUM Unq	105 UNNILPENTIUM Unp	106 UNNILHEXIUM Unh	107 UNNILSEPTIUM Uns	108 UNNILOCTIUM Uno	109 UNNILENNIUM Une

MENDELEEV'S PERIODIC TABLE 1869 • ELEMENT REACTION DEPENDS ON ELECTRONS

COMPOUNDS

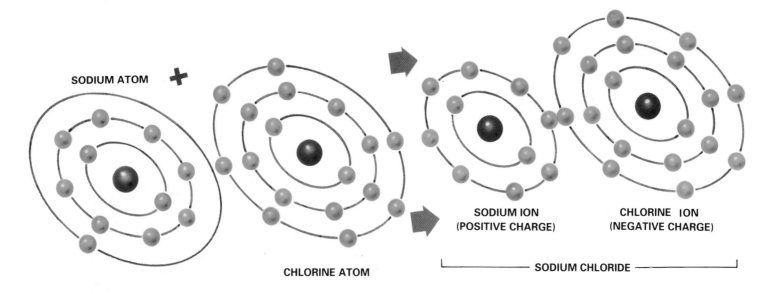

SODIUM ATOM +

CHLORINE ATOM

SODIUM ION (POSITIVE CHARGE)

CHLORINE ION (NEGATIVE CHARGE)

SODIUM CHLORIDE

Some chemical elements are more likely than others to react and form compounds. As we have seen, those in the left-hand group of the Periodic Table are the most reactive elements, while those in the right-hand group rarely react at all. The reactiveness of an element totally depends upon the location of the electrons inside its atoms.

Chemical Bonds

The electrons in an atom move around the central nucleus. Scientists think of them as occupying "shells", rather like the layers of an onion. Each shell can hold up to a certain number of electrons; the innermost shell, for example, can hold 2, and the next shell can have up to 8. Atoms are most stable when their shells are full. Neon, in the right-hand group, has 10 electrons which fill the first and second shells. It is very difficult to remove electrons from full shells.

The most reactive elements are those whose outer-most shell contains only a single electron. Sodium, for example, has a total of 11 electrons, 2 in the innermost shell, 8 in the second and 1 in the third. This lone electron can easily be removed from the atom, which means that sodium is highly reactive. The elements in the last-but-one group on the right of the table have outer shells that are one electron short. Chlorine, for instance, has only 7 electrons in its outer shell, which means it can easily take in another electron. Not surprisingly, sodium and chlorine atoms react strongly with each other to form a compound called sodium chloride, or common salt.

When an atom gains or loses an electron it becomes electrically charged. Electrons each carry a negative charge while protons have a positive charge, so having an extra electron creates a negatively charged atom and losing an electron creates a positively charged atom. Thus, when sodium loses an electron it gains a positive charge which is attracted to the negatively charged chlorine. Atoms that carry an electrical charge are called ions, and the attraction between oppositely charged ions is called an ionic bond.

Not all of the bonds that hold atoms or molecules together are ionic. Sometimes pairs of electrons can be

IONIC BONDS HAVE TRANSFER OF ELECTRONS • COVALENT BONDS SHARE ELECTRONS

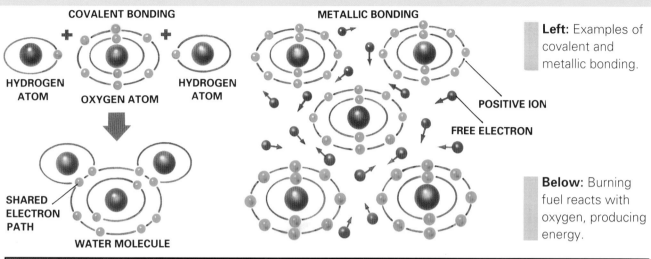

COVALENT BONDING

HYDROGEN ATOM

OXYGEN ATOM

HYDROGEN ATOM

SHARED ELECTRON PATH

WATER MOLECULE

METALLIC BONDING

POSITIVE ION

FREE ELECTRON

Left: Examples of covalent and metallic bonding.

Below: Burning fuel reacts with oxygen, producing energy.

shared between two atoms in what are called covalent bonds. Two chlorine atoms can share a pair of electrons, one from each, in order to fill their outer shells and make a stable chlorine molecule. A water molecule consists of a single oxygen atom sharing electrons with two hydrogen atoms.

The third type of chemical bonding is called metallic bonding. In a metal crystal, atoms lose some of their electrons and become positively charged ions. The lost electrons do not attach themselves to other atoms, but move around freely, rather like a "sea" of electrons that holds the metal ions together. These free-moving electrons help to explain why metals are good at conducting electricity and heat.

Reactions and Energy

When elements and compounds react to form new compounds, some molecules may be broken up and new ones created. These processes involve energy. Some reactions cannot start until extra energy is supplied in the form of heat. When coal (which is mainly carbon) burns it combines with oxygen in the air to form carbon dioxide. But coal will not start to burn unless it is heated. Other reactions may happen spontaneously and give off a great deal of energy. Sodium, for example, reacts very violently with water, giving off heat.

METALLIC BONDS HAVE "SEA" OF ELECTRONS • REACTIONS INVOLVE ENERGY CHANGES

EVOLUTION

The Earth was formed around 4,600 million years ago, and the first life forms appeared some time before 3,200 million years ago. Since that time, life on Earth has developed from the first primitive plants and animals into the huge variety of life forms that now inhabit our planet. How did this happen?

The Fossil Record

Until early in the nineteenth century, it was widely believed that all life on the planet had been created at the same time. This idea came from the story of the creation in the Bible, and some religious scholars had even calculated a precise date on which it happened, 4004 BC.

However, this theory was being challenged by evidence in the form of fossils. A fossil is the name given to any physical evidence of life that existed long ago. Most fossils are found in rocks, and they formed when plants or animals, for example, became buried in mud soon after their death and gradually turned to stone. As well as plants and animals, fossil footprints have been found, and even ripple marks that were made by water in the mud beneath ancient seas.

Around 200 years ago, people began discovering fossils of creatures that no longer existed. The first dinosaur fossils, for example, were found in England in 1822. These finds led scientists to question the story of the creation.

Darwin and Evolution

In 1859 the English scientist Charles Darwin published a book called *On the Origin of Species by Means of Natural Selection*. The theory behind it was that the life we now see on Earth is the result of many millions of years of development, or evolution. The idea of evolution was not new; a Frenchman, Jean-Baptiste de Lamarck, had suggested in 1806 that creatures evolved in order to improve themselves. Nonetheless, Darwin's book shook the scientific world to its foundations.

The basis of Darwin's theory is that living things evolve because of two factors: adaptation and natural selection. In a species with many millions of individual plants or animals, there are always some with characteristics or types of behaviour that are slightly different from the rest. Most of these differences are of no use, but some may give individuals in a particular environ-

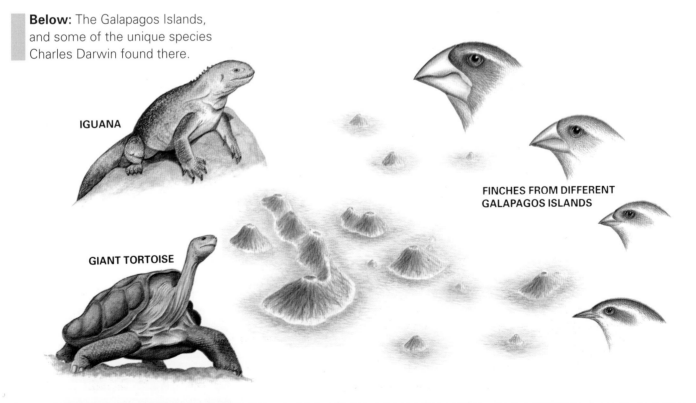

Below: The Galapagos Islands, and some of the unique species Charles Darwin found there.

IGUANA

GIANT TORTOISE

FINCHES FROM DIFFERENT GALAPAGOS ISLANDS

LAMARCK'S THEORY OF EVOLUTION 1806 • FIRST DINOSAUR FOSSIL IN ENGLAND 1822

ment an advantage over the rest of the species. These beneficial changes are called adaptations. Over countless generations an adaptation may spread throughout a species in a particular area. The result of this is that a new species is created, different from the one still living in other areas where the adaptations were not useful because they did not suit the environment there.

Since life began, countless new species have appeared on Earth, and countless more have disappeared, or become extinct. According to Darwin, the survival or extinction of a species is decided by natural selection, or the survival of the fittest. When a particular type of food is in short supply and there are a number of different species that depend upon it, some individuals may be better adapted to the job of obtaining food. For example, animals with a long neck are able to reach leaves several metres above the ground when all the food lower down has been eaten. This enables them to survive when creatures with short necks die out. Over many generations, the adaptation that produced a long neck spreads through the species, passing from parents to offspring.

Above: The fossil of a Pterodactyl dinosaur.

Below: Some extinct plants and animals.

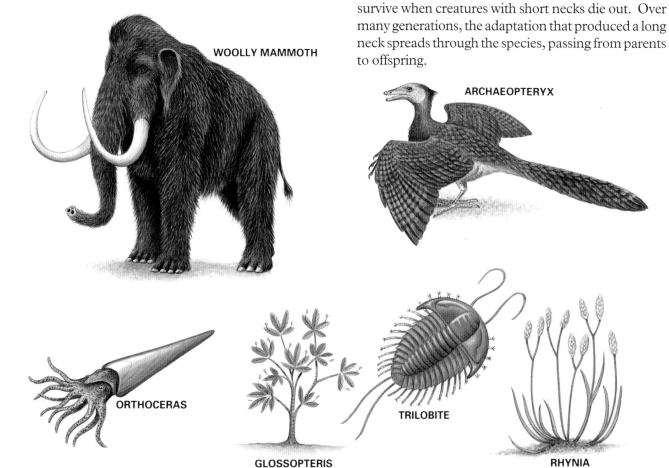

WOOLLY MAMMOTH

ARCHAEOPTERYX

ORTHOCERAS

GLOSSOPTERIS

TRILOBITE

RHYNIA

MEDICAL DISCOVERIES

Below: The microscope was one of the most important inventions in medical science. This early example of a compound microscope was made c.1680.

Of all the creatures that have inhabited the earth since life first began, humans are the only ones which are able to think about and try to improve their lives. This is especially true where illnesses and their cures are concerned.

Medicine is as old as human civilization itself, but the ancient Greeks were among the first people to look closely at the human body and its workings, and to write down what they discovered. Much of their knowledge was passed on to later civilizations, including the Romans, and one of the first great physicians was a Roman by the name of Galen.

Born in AD 130, Galen became the surgeon of Emperor Marcus Aurelius. Like the Greeks before him, he believed that the four basic elements of earth, air, fire and water were absorbed into the body as food and drink, and that they caused certain characteristics, or "humours" in human behaviour. Galen constructed a complicated theory to explain how the organs and tubes of the body worked. It involved what he called Natural Spirits which existed in the liver and turned food into blood, and Vital Spirits that enriched the blood when it reached the heart.

The Dawn of Modern Medicine

Despite his close observation of the human body, Galen failed to realize that blood is pumped around it by the heart. This fact was discovered by an Englishman, William Harvey, in 1628. He observed that the heart consists of muscles which expand and contract, allowing blood to enter and then forcing it out again.

In 1665 another important discovery was made. Looking through a microscope at a piece of cork (which is dead plant tissue), Robert Hooke saw tiny structures which he called cells. At about the same time the Dutchman Anton van Leeuwenhoek identified cells in blood. Eventually, in 1824, the French scientist René Dutrochet established that the tissue of all living things consists of cells.

Tools and Techniques

As in other areas of science, advances in medicine happened partly because new techniques and equipment were developed. The first thermometer for medical use was invented in 1626 by an Italian physician, Santorio. In 1761 an Austrian called Auenbrügger invented the technique of percussion. This allowed

doctors to detect the state of certain organs inside the body by tapping them with their fingers and listening to the sound. Sounds made by the body could be heard more accurately thanks to the invention of the stethoscope by René Laënnec in 1815. Four years later Jean-Louis Poiseuille invented the first manometer for measuring blood pressure.

Surgical operations were made much more bearable for patients by the invention of anaesthetics. Until the use of a gas called ether by C. W. Long in 1842, major surgery was agonisingly painful. Ether was later replaced by chloroform, which was first used by James Simpson in 1847.

One of the most important breakthroughs occurred even before those above, the invention of the microscope. No one is certain who invented it, but the first one was possibly made around 1600 by a Dutchman, Hans Jansen. In the 1660s Anton van Leeuwenhoek began grinding more accurate, powerful lenses which could magnify up to 300 times. As the science of making lenses improved over the years, microscopes were made which could be used to see smaller and smaller objects more clearly. One of the fields in which these microscopes enabled great advances to be made was microbiology.

Above: In 1628, William Harvey discovered the vital role of the heart as a pump that circulates blood in the body.

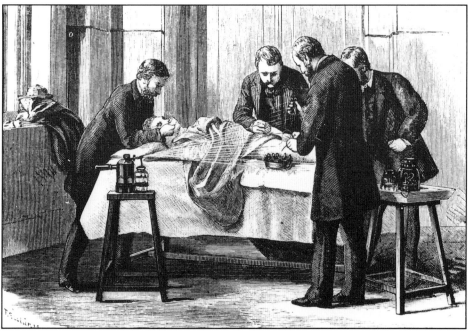

Left: A surgical operation in the 1860s. The patient has been anaesthetized with chloroform, which was first used in 1847.

FIRST MICROSCOPE MADE c.1600 • HOOKE AND LEEUWENHOEK DISCOVER CELLS 1665

MICROBIOLOGY

Below: In 1857 Louis Pasteur discovered that the air contains tiny living organisms, or microbes.

Microbiology is the study of tiny organisms such as bacteria and microbes. These organisms are too small to be seen with the naked eye, and microbiology only began after the invention of the microscope.

Louis Pasteur

The first person to discover micro-organisms was an Austrian doctor called Plenciz in 1762, but the real founder of microbiology was a French chemist, Louis Pasteur. In 1857 he was asked to find out why wine and other substances went bad when left exposed to the air. He discovered that the air contains tiny living things, which he called microbes. One of these, yeast, causes sugar to ferment into alcohol and makes bread rise. Others, germs or bacteria, make food go bad.

Pasteur also found that the microbes could be killed by heat, and much of the milk we drink today is heat-treated in this way, using a process called pasteurization.

Pasteur's discovery led on to the work of Joseph Lister, an English surgeon. He was appalled by the number of patients whose wounds became infected when the skin was broken, either in an accident or during surgery. Realizing that Pasteur's microbes might be responsible, from 1867 he devised methods of killing the germs responsible for infection and keeping them out of wounds. Without Lister's so-called antiseptic techniques, many of the surgical operations that we now take for granted would be impossible.

A German scientist, Robert Koch, made another important breakthrough in 1883, when he discovered the bacteria which cause two dangerous diseases in humans -tuberculosis and cholera. Further progress in the fight against disease came in 1898 when Martinus Beijerinck found micro-organisms that are even smaller than bacteria and can attack living cells from the inside. They are called viruses. Many viruses are too small to be seen even with an ordinary microscope, and could not be identified until the invention of the electron microscope in 1933.

The Battle Against Disease

As well as identifying the causes of serious diseases, scientists are also concerned about finding out how to

Right: Edward Jenner's use in 1786 of cowpox vaccine to prevent smallpox caused much hilarity. However, it was very successful, and smallpox has now been wiped out all over the world.

Below right: Joseph Lister, whose antiseptic techniques protected patients undergoing surgery against infections caused by germs.

cure or prevent them. The first important step in this direction came in 1786, even before the cause of the disease smallpox was known. An English doctor, Edward Jenner, noticed that people who had suffered from a mild form of smallpox, known as cowpox, never caught smallpox itself. He smeared a boy's arm with the liquid from cowpox blisters and then scratched the skin. Several months later he injected the boy with smallpox. The cowpox "vaccine" had made the boy immune to both cowpox and smallpox. Thanks to Jenner's discovery, smallpox has now been completely wiped out all over the world.

In 1885 Louis Pasteur vaccinated a man who had been bitten by a dog that had rabies. His experiment was a success and the man survived. Pasteur's contribution to the study of diseases did not end there. He suggested that humans and other living things had inside them cells that can fight diseases by attacking the microbes which cause them. Over the years he has been proved correct, and scientists are continually finding out more about the body's immune system.

JENNER VACCINATES AGAINST SMALLPOX 1786 • BEIJERINCK DISCOVERS VIRUSES 1898

GENETICS AND DNA

Have you ever noticed that children look like one or other of their parents in some ways? Perhaps you have some of the same characteristics as your own mother or father, the same colour eyes, similar facial features, or long or short fingers, for example. The passing-on of characteristics like these from parents to offspring is called heredity, and it is studied in the science of genetics.

Gregor Mendel

In 1866 Gregor Mendel, a monk in part of what is now Czechoslovakia, published the results of experiments he had carried out on garden pea plants. He had identified seven different characteristics, including shape of seed, colour of seed and length of stem, and had crossed plants with the same characteristics to see what sort of plants they produced.

At that time, it was believed that the offspring of animals or plants had characteristics halfway between those of their parents. Mendel proved otherwise. He found that when plants with tall stems were crossed with others having the same characteristic, most of the new plants would also have tall stems, but a quarter of them would have short stems.

His theory was that each characteristic is decided by two particles which are present in each plant. In tall plants, for example, there is one particle producing tallness and another producing shortness, but the tallness particle is "dominant", or more likely to be passed on. Therefore, a tallness particle from one plant crossed with a similar particle from another will give rise to another tall plant. Likewise, a tallness particle crossed with a shortness particle will also give a tall plant, because tallness is dominant. But when two shortness particles come together, as they do once in every four crossings, they produce a short plant.

Genes and DNA

We now call these particles genes. This was the name given to them in 1910 by Thomas Hunt Morgan, an American who experimented on heredity among fruit flies in much the same way as Mendel had with peas. Genes are contained in thread-like structures called chromosomes, found in the nucleus at the centre of each living cell.

The remaining mystery was how the information contained in genes of parents is passed on to their

Below: Through his experiments with pea plants, Gregor Mendel discovered how physical characteristics are passed from parents to their offspring. The same principle can be seen in the diagram, which shows how eye colour is inherited.

MOTHER
● RECESSIVE GENE
● DOMINANT GENE
FATHER
CHILDREN

Below: When a cell divides, its DNA breaks down to form matched pairs of chromosomes.

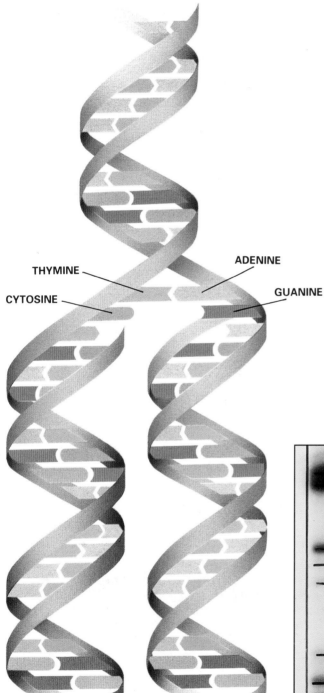

THYMINE

CYTOSINE

ADENINE

GUANINE

offspring. This question was solved in 1953 by Francis Crick and James Watson. They looked closely at a complicated molecule called deoxyribonucleic acid, or DNA, from which chromosomes are made. They found that it consists of long chains, each in the form of two interlocking spirals, made up of four different chemicals. Genes are made up of groups of these chemicals arranged in specific positions.

Living cells multiply by dividing in two. Each half becomes a new cell which grows and divides again. When a cell divides, the DNA in the nucleus breaks down and forms paired segments, chromosomes. All cells, except those responsible for reproduction, contain paired sets of chromosomes which carry all the information that is needed to make a particular organism. The reproduction cells contain only half of the information needed, and the complete "picture" can only be made by combining one cell from a male with one from a female.

The DNA of every individual animal and plant is different from all others. Because of this, scientists can now identify people by examining the DNA in, for example, their blood cells. This technique, called genetic fingerprinting, was developed in Britain in 1985 by Alec Jeffreys.

Below: Genetic fingerprinting; the pattern of bands is different for everyone, but people who are related have some similar bands.

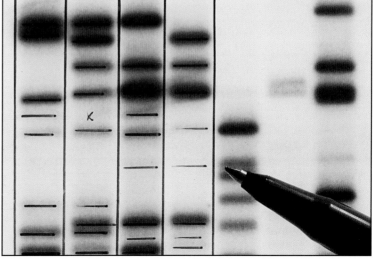

CRICK & WATSON UNRAVEL DNA DOUBLE HELIX 1953 • GENETIC FINGERPRINTING 1985

MODERN INNOVATIONS

During the last hundred years or so, medicine has advanced in leaps and bounds. Scientists and doctors have been able to find out exactly how diseases and other ailments affect the body, and have devised new methods of detecting, treating, and curing many of them.

One of the most well-known inventions is a drug called acetylsalicylic acid, or aspirin. It was first made in 1853, but was not recognized as a pain-killer until 40 years later. Furthermore, doctors have discovered recently that aspirin is also good for the heart if taken in moderate quantities.

Another invention benefiting the heart was made in 1958. The pacemaker, devised by Swedish doctor Ake Senning, can be implanted into a heart that is not beating correctly. The device supplies tiny electrical impulses to make the heart beat evenly and at the correct speed.

Sometimes the heart can become diseased. In exceptional cases, the disease may become so severe that the heart can no longer function, and doctors may carry out a heart transplant operation. This involves removing the diseased heart and replacing it with a healthy one from a suitable donor. The first heart transplant was carried out in 1967 by Dr Christiaan Barnard. It is also possible to transplant other organs, including the liver and kidneys.

Some of the most frequently used drugs are antibiotics. Made from micro-organisms, they work by attacking and destroying other micro-organisms, the bacteria and fungi that cause diseases. The first antibiotic, penicillin, was discovered by Alexander Fleming in 1928.

Medical Detectives

Röntgen's discovery of X-rays in 1895 immediately found a use in medicine. Because these rays pass through body tissue more easily than bone, it is possible to see broken or damaged bones in X-ray "photographs". In recent years, machines called scanners have been developed which can be used to view internal organs. The X-ray scanner was perfected in 1972 by Godfrey Hounsfield. Other types of scanner use radio waves or ultrasound (high-frequency sound waves). Ultrasound scanners are often used to examine unborn babies in the mother's womb.

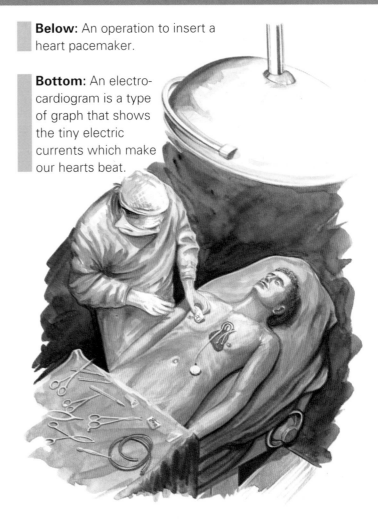

Below: An operation to insert a heart pacemaker.

Bottom: An electro-cardiogram is a type of graph that shows the tiny electric currents which make our hearts beat.

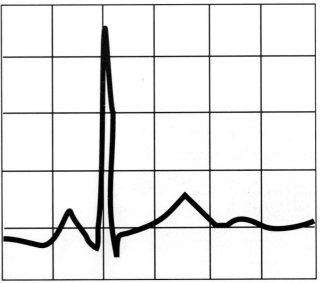

ASPIRIN FIRST USED 1893 • PENICILLIN 1928 • RADIOTHERAPY 1934 • PACEMAKER 1958

The Fight Against Cancer

There are a number of different types of cancer, affecting various parts of the body, but they all damage the body in much the same way. When an abnormal cell forms in the body, it sometimes multiplies quickly to form a tumour. If the tumour grows large enough, it can prevent an internal organ from working. Cancer cells can break free from a tumour and travel through the bloodstream to other parts of the body, where they start new tumours.

Until the discovery of X-rays, and of artificial radioactivity in 1934, there was no method of treating cancer. Doctors can now kill cancer cells by bombarding them with X-rays and gamma rays, which are aimed very carefully so that few healthy cells are damaged at the same time. This technique, known as radiotherapy, was first used effectively in 1934.

Another means of killing tumours was developed in 1964. It is called chemotherapy, and involves using very strong drugs to attack the cancer cells. Thanks to these two treatments, most cancers can now be cured if they are detected early enough.

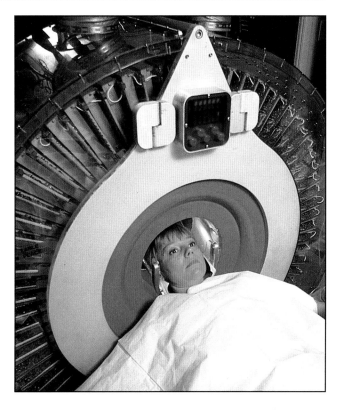

Above: A patient undergoing a brain scan. Scanners like this are often used to detect tumours in the brain.

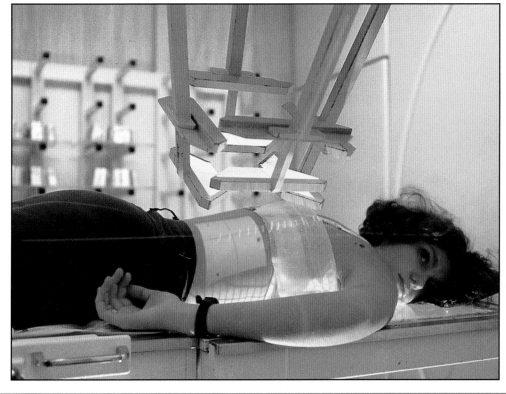

Left: Laser beams are used to ensure that a patient's body is positioned correctly prior to radiotherapy.

NUMBERS

Mathematics is the name for a group of sciences which includes algebra, geometry and calculus. It is concerned with the study of the quantity and shape of things, how much space they occupy, and the links between these factors.

Mathematics is vital to all other sciences, because it gives scientists a way of expressing their theories, recording and analysing the results of experiments, and explaining their conclusions. Perhaps most important of all is the fact that the "language" of mathematics (the signs and symbols that are used and the way in which calculations are written down) is international: one scientist can read and understand the mathematical calculations of another, even though they may live on opposite sides of the world and be unable to speak each other's language.

The First Numbers

Numbers have a central part to play in the language of mathematics. The quantity of something is expressed as a number: mass, speed, height and many other ways of describing objects are written as a number and a unit of measurement, 25g, 200 km/h, 46 m, for example.

Numbers were first used in writing about 5,000 years ago. Clay tablets found in the ruins of ancient cities in Mesopotamia and Persia are inscribed with symbols representing both words and numbers. From around 500 BC, the Mayan civilization in Central America developed a number system based on counting in twenties, the combined number of fingers and toes. At about the same time, the ancient Greeks began using the letters of the alphabet to represent numbers. Their system was used for a thousand years, and was adapted by both the Hebrews and the Arabs.

In Babylonia during the fourth century BC, a new symbol began to appear, the symbol for zero. Until then, the idea of there being none of something was represented by a space in a row or column of figures.

In the third century BC, certain special numbers were discovered by the Greeks. The mathematician Euclid realized that there were some numbers, called prime numbers, which can only be divided by 1 and themselves. For example, the only whole numbers (not

MODERN ARABIC	1	2	3	4	5	6	7	8	9	10	100
EGYPTIAN	I	II	III	IIII	II/III	III/III	IIII/III	IIII/IIII	III/III/III	∩	℮
HINDU	?	૨	૩	૪	૫	૬	૭	૮	૩	?°	?°°
BABYLONIAN	▼	▼▼	▼▼▼	▼▼▼▼	▼▼▼/▼▼	▼▼▼/▼▼▼	▼▼▼▼/▼▼▼	▼▼▼▼/▼▼▼▼	▼▼▼▼▼/▼▼▼▼	➤	▼⪯
ROMAN	I	II	III	IIII	V	VI	VII	VIII	IX	X	C
MAYAN	•	••	•••	••••	—	•/—	••/—	•••/—	••••/—	═	(shell)

fractions) by which 11 can be divided are 1 and 11 itself. Therefore 11 is a prime number whereas 12, which can be divided by 1, 2, 3, 4, 6 and 12, is not. The largest prime number so far discovered was found by accident in 1985, with the aid of a supercomputer. It is a staggering 65,050 digits long.

The Modern System

The development of our modern system of numbers began in India around 1,500 years ago. For the first time, numbers were represented by just ten figures, from 0 to 9, as used today. Numbers greater than 9 were shown by combining figures and placing them in what are called decimal positions. For example, in the number 2,365, the right-hand position shows single units (ones), the next position is for tens, the next for hundreds, and so on.

In 829 the Arab scientist Mohammad Ibn Musa al-Khwarizmi adopted this system, and its use was later spread to Europe. However, the ten figures were not always written in the same way. When the printing press was invented around 1440, it was possible to fix the exact shapes of the figures so that everyone used the same ones.

Below: Roman numerals are very popular. Here we see them used on a clock face.

Left: Some examples of ancient number systems, together with the equivalent arabic numerals we use today.

MODERN SYSTEM BEGINS IN INDIA FIFTH CENTURY AD • REACHES EUROPE c.980

GEOMETRY

We saw in the previous chapter how numbers were first used and how our modern number system was developed. The area of mathematics which deals with numbers and numerical calculations (addition, subtraction, multiplication and division) is called arithmetic. If you look around, you will see that the world consists not of numbers but of shapes, which are made up of straight lines, curves and surfaces. The study of these shapes is called geometry.

Early Geometry

The earliest practical uses of geometry were in building. When a temple, for example, was being constructed, its builders needed to know whether or not the ground was level and the walls vertical. From the time of the world's first cities, which grew up around 5,500 years ago, builders have used devices such as set squares (triangles in which one angle is a right angle) to help them build walls at 90° to the ground. The ancient Egyptians knew how to make a number of these right-angled triangles, with sides of various lengths. (The simplest has sides of 3, 4 and 5 units.) The Babylonians probably knew many more.

In the seventh century BC, the Greek mathematician Thales devised a clever way of measuring the height of buildings and other objects. He measured the shadow cast by the object when the sun was at an angle of 45° (half of a right angle) in the sky, because he had calculated that the length of the shadow would then be the same as the height of the object.

Pythagoras and Euclid

The person who did most to advance the science of geometry was Pythagoras, a Greek mathematician of the sixth century BC. He looked at right-angled triangles and asked himself what makes them special. What is the relationship between the lengths of the three sides? The answer he arrived at is known as Pythagoras' Theorem. It states that "the square of the hypotenuse is equal to the sum of the squares on the other two sides". Or, to put it more simply, if the length of the hypotenuse (the longest side of the triangle which faces the right angle) is squared (multiplied by itself), the number this makes will equal the square of one of the remaining sides added to the square of the other. In a simple 3,4,5 right-angled triangle, for example, the hypotenuse is 5 units long. When it is squared (5 x 5)

it makes 25. The squares of the other two sides are 9 (3 x 3) and 16 (4 x 4), which add up to 25. Pythagoras' Theorem is true for every triangle that contains a right angle, and it has been called the most important single theorem in the whole of mathematics.

One of the most famous names in geometry is that of Euclid, a Greek who lived in Alexandria from about 300 BC. He gathered together the work of earlier mathematicians, including Pythagoras, and organized it into an orderly system. His book, *Elements of Geometry*, has been translated and copied more times than any other book apart from the Bible. It was still being used to teach geometry at the beginning of this century.

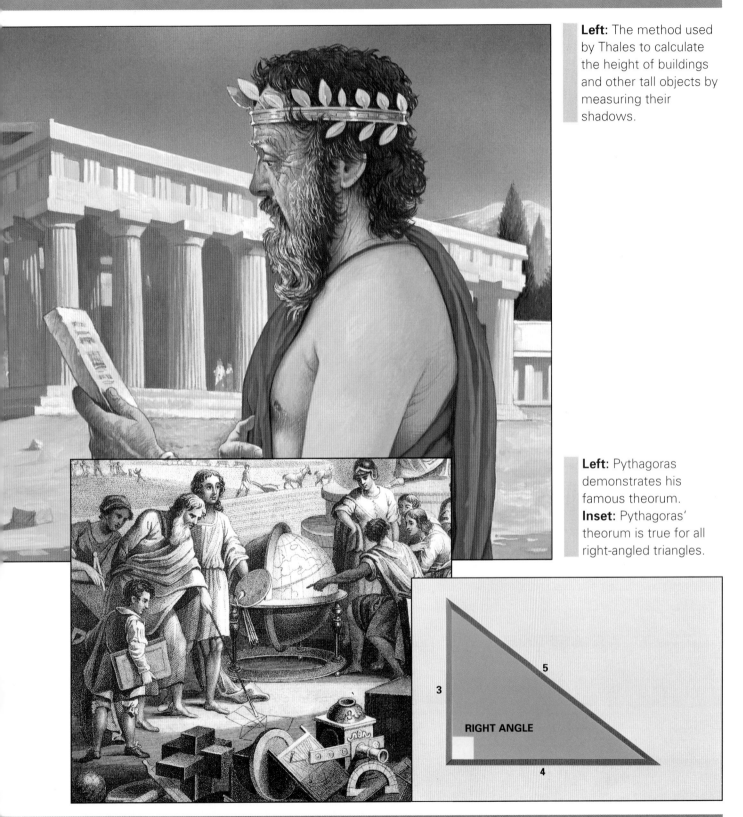

Left: The method used by Thales to calculate the height of buildings and other tall objects by measuring their shadows.

Left: Pythagoras demonstrates his famous theorum.
Inset: Pythagoras' theorum is true for all right-angled triangles.

3

5

RIGHT ANGLE

4

PYTHAGORAS' THEOREM FOR RIGHT-ANGLED TRIANGLES c.550 BC • EUCLID c.300 BC

ALGEBRA

Algebra is a branch of mathematics. It is rather like a special language in which symbols are used to represent numbers and quantities. Many of these symbols are letters of the alphabet. These letters are often used to represent unknown quantities. Arithmetical signs, such as + and - for addition and subtraction, are also used, and so are ordinary numbers.

Signs and Equations

The ancient Egyptians had signs for addition and subtraction: in their hieroglyphic writing, two legs walking in the same direction meant the same as our plus sign, while two legs walking in opposite directions meant minus. The signs we use today were originally developed in the fifteenth, sixteenth and seventeenth centuries. Although the origins of algebra date back to the third century in Alexandria, Egypt, the first important developments were made by two Frenchmen, Pierre de Fermat and François Viète. In 1591, in his book *Ars analytica*, Viète first devised the language of algebra that is still used today.

Algebra is used as a means of describing the relationships between things, and using these relationships to calculate unknown quantities from known ones. This is done using what are called equations. These are rather like mathematical versions of the sentences you use when speaking, except that they contain numbers and letters instead of words. You might have guessed from the spelling of the word equation that it has something to do with being equal. Equations are written in such a way that the quantities on both sides are equal, as in a simple equation such as $n + 8 = 20$. The unknown quantity, n, can be calculated by solving the equation. In solving equations, you can use addition, subtraction, multiplication and division, but you must always do the same thing to both sides of an equation to make sure that they stay equal. The aim is to get the unknown quantity, n, on its own on one side of the equation. For example, to solve $n + 8 = 20$, you can subtract 8 from each side, making $n = 20 - 8$. You can then see that n equals 12.

ALGEBRA ORIGINATES IN THIRD-CENTURY ALEXANDRIA • FRANÇOIS VIÈTE (1540-1603)

Above: Part of an Egyptian mathematical papyrus from about 1575 BC.

Below: François Viète (1540-1603) was the founder of modern algebra.

Solving Practical Problems

Equations can be used to solve problems in everyday life. Perhaps you are planning to go on a car journey with your parents. If the petrol tank holds x litres and the car can travel y kilometres for every litre, you will be able to go z kilometres before stopping for petrol. Each litre takes you y km and you have x litres, so you can go x x y km, which is written as xy. You know the distance is z, so you can write $xy = z$. So long as you know two of these three quantities, you can solve the equation. If x is 36 litres and y is 12 km per litre, x x y, (which equals z) is 36 x 12, or 432 km. If your journey will be longer than 432 km, you will need more petrol.

You can also use equations to work out how much things cost. If a 5kg bag of potatoes costs a certain amount of money, you can calculate how much each kg costs, and compare it with the price of, say, a 3kg bag.

Many equations are much more complicated than the ones we have looked at, but they are just as useful when it comes to solving difficult problems in science.

LANGUAGE OF ALGEBRA DEVELOPED BY VIÈTE 1591 • PIERRE DE FERMAT (1601-1665)

INDEX

ACKNOWLEDGEMENTS

The publishers would like to thank the following organizations and individuals for their kind permission to reproduce the pictures in this book:

Allsport/Gary Mortimore 10, /Christian Petit Vandystadt 11; Ancient Art and Architecture Collection 77; Astro Art/David A. Hardy 57; Colorsport/Gromik Thierry 61; Stephen Gorton 33 (bottom); The Hulton Picture Company 65 (bottom); The Hutchinson Library/Jeremy A Horner 27; The Octopus Group Picture Library 52 (right), 53 (left); Rex Features/Sipa Press 59; Ann Ronan Picture Library 23, 37, 45, 52 (left), /E. P. Goldschmidt & Co. 53 (right), /Ann Ronan 67 (bottom), 75, 77; Science Photo Library 8, 23, 34, 35, /Almos National Laboratory 51, /Peter Aprahamian 15, /BSIP Boucharlat 71 (bottom), /J. L. Charmet 43, 49, 67 (top), /Dr. Ray Clark & Mervyn Goff front cover (centre), /CNRI 39, /Martin Dohrn 30, /Hencoup Enterprises 55, /Dr. Mike McNamee 6, /Peter Menzel 16, /Hank Morgan 71 (top), /NASA 13, 21, /David Parker 29, 69, /Alfred Pasteka front cover (right), /STC A. Sternberg 47 (bottom), /Sinclair Stammers 63, /St. Bartholomews Hospital 65 (top), /David Taylor 41, /U. S. Library of Congress 31, /Brik Viktor 54; Tony Stone Worldwide/Stephen Johnson 47 (inset); University of Pennsylvania/The Science Museum, London 47 (top).

Illustrations by:

Wayne Ford - pages 39. 62, 63
Kevin Jones (Artist Partners) - pages 25, 74-75
Joe Lawrence - pages 9, 14, 17, 20-21, 26-27, 29, 32, 38, 46, 50, 54, 72-73
The Maltings Partnership - pages 7, 11, 13, 15, 16, 18-19, 22-23, 24, 28, 30-31, 35, 36, 42-43, 44-45, 48-49, 56-57, 58-59, 60-61, 64, 69, 70 (top), 75 (below), 76
Finbar O'Connor - pages 12, 37, 40, 53, 66, 68

Mark Summersby - page 70 (below)
Illustrations in top right-hand corners by Joe Lawrence.

The illustrations in the top right-hand corners of the right-hand pages in this book show the following:

Page 7, garnet; page 9, nucleus of an atom; page 11, inclined plane and ball; page 13, an apple; page 15, floating iceberg; page 17, a spring; page 19, a see-saw; page 21, an oil rig; page 23, a steaming kettle; page 25, Von Guericke's vacuum sphere; page 27, the Sun; page 29, reflection; page 31, a light bulb; page 33, an eye; page 35, an X-ray machine; page 37, a guitar; page 39, a bat; page 41, a fork of lightening; page 43, a battery; page 45, a magnet; page 47, a computer; page 49, a radioactive symbol; page 51, a neutron bombarding a nucleus; page 53, Saturn; page 55, a radiotelescope; page 57, a spiral galaxy; page 59, a gold nugget; page 61, a water molecule; page 63, early ape and early man; page 65, a stethoscope; page 67, bacteria microbes; page 69, carbon molecules; page 71, an antibiotic capsule; page 73, early Egyptian numbers; page 75, a compass; page 77, the mathematical symbol X.